COUPONS MADE EZ

BASIC PRINCIPLES OF COUPONING

Contents

COPYWRITE

Coupons Made EZ
Copyright: Showeet Blyther
ISBN-10: 1523890010
Published: 02/19/15
Publisher: create space
Kindle Edition

To find out more please visit www.couponsmadeez.com or couponsmadeez@gmail.com; Twitter/Instagram/ Facebook CouponsMadeEZ

Preface and Acknowledgement
This book is dedicated to my loving husband
Maurice Blyther and my three beautiful girls
Serenity, Semaiah and Sea 'Ana. I love you
forever and ever with my entire heart.

I want to thank my parents Lidia Schaefer and Larry Pope for bringing me into this world. I want to thank my beautiful mother for raising me all by herself and making many selfless sacrifices. I want to thank my Pastors Dr. Michael Freeman and Dr. Deloris Freeman [affectionately known as Dr. Deedee] for teaching me to that this is the year of realized dreams. I also want to thank Dr. Deedee for the nudge to get this book written; I am almost certain this would not have come to pass if she had not stirred up the gift in me to get it done. I am forever grateful for the teaching ministry of Spirit of Faith Christian Center. I would also like to thank Carolyn S. Jones for editing my book; I could not have done this without you.

ABOUT THE AUTHOR ~

My name is Showeet Blyther. My first name comes from my mother's homeland of Ethiopia. When I was younger I hated that name because so many kids would tease and make fun of me. My name means "fresh harvest." I have learned to love my name, realizing that it's the best thing my mom has ever given me other than life.

I am the wife of one man for over fourteen years and the mother of three beautiful girls. I have been a stay at home mom on and off for the most part of our marriage. Before we got married, I agreed to stay home when we had children. We thought it was a great idea, however, my mother raised a strong independent woman. I have always worked prior to my marriage; and I wasn't "Betty Crocker." I have since learned to cook; and I mean cook really good, along the way. However, there has always been a struggle for me to be a stay at home parent. I would get a job, keep it for two years or less, and then quit. It just didn't work with our family dynamics. Plus, the cost of child care was/is ridiculous, and that is where most of my pay check went. I was so frustrated with the desire to work; however, it just wasn't working out the way I had planned. My husband couldn't understand my desire to work because we did agree that I would stay home with our children.

When I learned the art of *couponing*, it became my purpose as a stay at home parent. A part of me always wanted to bring money into our household because I've always wanted to help. However, I had an "ah-ha" moment when I realized that I was so focused on bringing money in and I wasn't thinking of how I could "keep" the money in our household. This concept of keeping money in was major. It was like a light bulb went off in my head. Coupons became the answer and it continues to help us keep money in our household. The money that we would typically spend on our daily needs can now be saved for other things. I haven't thought about working one day since I began couponing. I treat couponing like a part time job and it's rewarding too!

I have always wondered how to coupon. Many years ago, I worked for Giant Food I watched in awe at my customers' amounts drop close to zero or often times actually drop to zero. When I asked about how to coupon, no one ever gave me a complete answer. I was always told, "Oh these coupons are in the Sunday paper" or "I printed this online," however, I wanted a step by step detailed explanation. I wanted a complete breakdown, and none of the couponing customers would grant this request. It took me more than 14 years to figure it out for myself. That doesn't mean that I've been searching for answers for that entire time. To be honest, I never really took the time to investigate or learn the strategies of couponing. I really just wanted someone to tell me how to coupon. I thought that would be easier for me to grasp. It actually just took a friend to give me some coupons and tell me where to go and get more coupons that began my quest for extreme couponing.

My friend Kimberly (Kimmie) Daniels gave me the information I needed to be successful. She gave me a stack of her extra coupons and a gift basket of all her freebie items. That basket gave me so much motivation because I was able to see with my own eyes what she told me she paid nickels, pennies and dimes for. That was all the motivation I needed to start gathering up my own research on the art of couponing. My hope is that this book does the same for you; give you the motivation to start couponing so that you are able to save money on your grocery bill.

Many people ask me how to coupon. I spend my time and energy telling them and they never get started. I want you to start, be successful, and to never pay retail price again on your grocery bill.

LET'S GET STARTED ~

Let me start out by telling you NOW, couponing requires a lot of research and planning if you plan to be successful. I want you to be successful and it is possible. Yes, it does take time to build what we couponers like to call stockpiles. I can almost guarantee that if you take the time, do the homework, and make a plan, you will find that in the end it was indeed well worth it; especially if it costs, pennies, nickels, and dimes.

So let's imagine that we are doing a puzzle for a quick second. When you assemble a puzzle, you must complete it piece by piece until it's finished. Now you can do smaller puzzles in minutes, but when you get the 5000 or larger piece puzzles, it may take days. The same goes for stockpiling. You stock up items piece by piece. One-day toothpaste, the next couple of days' body wash, the next month may be cereal, tuna, and bleach. It is completely random. One never knows what coupons and specials the newspaper inserts may contain or what product item the stores will have on sale. It's best to be prepared and organized.

In this book, you will learn how to coupon, where to get coupons, and how to obtain coupons directly from the manufacturers. Located in the back of this book are a couple of store policies on couponing. If you need to locate more stores coupon policies go directly to the store's website and search "coupon policies." I made this book small enough to go in your purse, book bag, or diaper bag so you are able to use it whenever you have any questions.

Let this book become your couponing manual. Flip to the store you need when you need it. Located in the back of this book are also the numbers to customer service for each store mentioned. Now there will be times when you cannot rectify a situation directly with management. Always maintain a peaceful disposition with management and call the corporate office to tell them the issue at hand. They will be more than happy to rectify the issue before you leave the store.

My mother said get a good education, because no one can ever take that from you. I agree with that statement. I am saying the same thing here in regards to coupons. Get a clear understanding of coupons and how to use them effectively, and no one will ever be able to take that away for you. I see couponing as a life skill that can be carried out from one generation to the next. Once you get a clear understanding you will always have food on the table.

Once in my life I wondered how we would feed our children. I filled out every application the government had and was told that my husband made too much money. The government doesn't consider the cost of your mortgage, water bill, electric bill, car note, car insurance, health insurance, telephone bill, and all the other bills you have. I had just had a baby; my husband broke his leg, and things where super tight in our finances. Food was the last thing on the list of things that needed to be paid. We needed a roof over our head, we needed the car, the insurance to drive the car. . . you get where I'm going with this?

After the delivery of my baby, my friends asked if there was anything they could do for us. My answer was always, "Yes, can you cook us a meal?" They didn't know that meal was the only meal that sustained us. My husband couldn't walk or drive, and neither could I because I had a cesarean section and two older children who needed food. I am so glad that struggle is over. I thank GOD for those families that cooked for us and I will be forever grateful.

However, I didn't like the feeling of the unknown; what will we eat tomorrow? We never went a day without food, and GOD kept us just like HE tells us in the bible. If this is you and you are in this place, follow this book and I promise you, you will always have food to eat. It may not be what you want, but if you have to make what you have work, I suggest you learn to get creative in the area of cooking. If you need further assistance, use the World Wide Web as a tool for recipes. I would like to also suggest that you purchase a crock pot for the convenience of a home cooked meal while you're away from home grabbing those deals with your coupons.

STOCKPILING ~

To give you an idea of how your stockpile will look, I will tell you what I currently have in my three freezers. Yes, I have three freezers and I'm in need of another but that's a different story.

I have hot dogs, lunch meat, bacon, meatballs, chicken nuggets, stuffed chicken breast, pancakes, waffles, toaster strudels, bread, frozen vegetables, French fries, frozen potatoes, onion rings, and pizza.

My personal care items consist of body washes, bar soaps, lotions, shampoos, conditioners, razors, deodorants, toilet tissue, paper towels, facial tissue, maxi pads, tampons, toothpaste, mouth wash, nail polish, band aids, sun screen, makeup, facial soap, facial cream and hairspray.

My laundry care items consist of laundry detergents, stain remover and bleach. Cleaning products consist of window sprays, floor cleaner, multi surface cleaner, multi surface wipes, toilet cleaners, toilet fresher's, air freshness, candles and plug-ins.

Snacks consist of yogurt, pudding, crackers, nut bars, granola bars, cookies, chips, multiple varieties of candy.

Food items include multiple brands of cereal, cheese, oatmeal, tuna fish, barbecue sauce, ketchup, hot sauce, mustard, mayonnaise, rice, pasta, pasta sauce, coffee, coffee creamer, and beans.

Everything I just mentioned was purchased with coupons. That's how I live; if we don't have a coupon we can't have it. Except for items like fresh meat and produce. It is not because we don't have money for it, it just doesn't make sense for me to pay full price for any products. You must have willpower to say no, even to yourself. My children know not to ask for random items; well, they still do but my response is, "Do we have a coupon for that?"

SECURING YOUR STOCKPILE:

If you live in an apartment I suggest you purchase dark colored storage bins to keep your stockpile out of site. I have heard stories of items being stolen from people who live in apartments allegedly from maintenance workers. Place your items inside the dark storage bins and place a table cover over it and put a lamp on top...be creative. If you live in a home, I suggest placing your items in a room that only the people who live with you may enter. Create your stockpile in an extra room upstairs, basement or attack. This will prohibit every visitor from asking for items from your stockpile. My husband is an ex police officer current sheriff deputy he always says burglaries occur because the place has already been surveilled. Meaning robbers know who to rob because they have seen the goods. I suggest skipping the idea of posting every deal on social media. Some of your friends are there because they support you, some of the people are there to jump on an opportunity. I have a sharp shooter in my house plus two pit bulls and I still refrain from showing my hauls on social media. Use wisdom in this area, the above mentioned are suggestions. I know you're thinking who would steal simple items as soap, toothpaste, and laundry detergent? It happens every day at stores all across the land. These stores have security and they catch thieves every day.

I would also suggest shelving for storage. I like my stuff neat and lined up in proper order. I know that's just me, but you will need a place for your new stuff and I just wanted to give you a heads up.

Examples Below of Free Items I Acquired with Coupons ~

Freebies here!!! Always look for sales like this when you have a 75 cents coupon.

COUPONS CYCLE BACK AROUND ~

When I first got started no one told me that the coupons come and go in cycles. This means you will see the coupon again; this is true on many products that you will see in the coupon inserts as well as internet printed coupons.

This is how couponers build stock piles. They purchase the same items that occur in the weekly inserts over and over as they continue to find the same sales over and over. That is how a stock pile grows. Rome was not built in one day and neither will your stockpile grow.

In the beginning, every sale I saw was chased with all I had. I actually went after every deal! I didn't want to miss anything; I just wouldn't allow myself to miss a deal. I was acting like a crazy lady, missing sleep and everything. I would rather coupon than enjoy life. I didn't want to go out with friends or family. In my mind, I would rather coupon. I did not want to miss not one deal.

I remember when I was so disappointed during my first super double. (I will explain super double later in the book.) I couldn't get this particular brand of body wash. Every day I went to the store and this brand of body wash was sold out. Now mind you most sales last for seven days. I went to that store for seven days straight; more than one time a day. I wasn't able to purchase that brand of body wash and I was aggravated! I spent all that time cutting, planning, and driving to that store for seven days without being able to get the prize at the end. This will happen, and it's ok when the store is out of stock; simply grab a rain check and always ask for the maximum permitted. Most of the time it's six per rain check. If you go to that store every day and they are out of stock every day, you should get rain check every day. The next week the same brand of body wash was on sale at another store. I had to pay a little more but at least I got it and I was satisfied. The hunt of that body wash took over my natural mind. I was a tiger and the body wash was my prey. I had never used this brand of body wash in my life, but I just had to have it. When I used it, I discovered it was nothing more special about this brand of soap than other brand. Lesson learned: you will miss a deal, but don't beat yourself up. The coupons will come around again, and another sale will resurface.

BRANDING ~

I want to discuss with you briefly the term, "branding." Companies spend big money to keep you as a customer. Do you have a favorite brand of chips? Is the salt vs. chip ratio super perfect? Does your mouth water up when you see them? Is this brand of chip a must have? Do you know the theme song to your favorite brand of chips? Have your purchased the same brand of chip year after year?

Now allow me to ask you another set of questions: Do they pay you to eat those chips? Do they offer you coupons for these chips? Do they give you any kind of discounts for purchasing these chips?

Let me deprogram you!! Yes, you have been programmed by their million-dollar marketing department. As a couponer, you must let branding go! Yes, let it go! I have all brands in my home and my current brand is "coupon brand". Before I started couponing I purchased the same brand year after year. They had me; I didn't even realize it either. Go outside of your norm, and you may just find out you like other brands. My ultimate goal for you is to enjoy "coupon brands". Now maybe you have skin allergies and you can only use sensitive skin products. Many products have products for people with sensitive skin. Or maybe you're not sure how your skin would do with new products like laundry detergent or body soap. In that case, purchase the sensitive skin type in all the brands until you can determine how a product will affect your skin. There are many ways to go around this; you just have to be creative. Also if you purchase something like body wash and you don't like the scent or it doesn't go with your body type, use that same soap for hand soap in the guest bathroom, or wash the dog with it. You can also make gift baskets for your family members. Conditioner is a great substitute for shaving cream. Remember you must be creative, I will repurpose products in other ways because everything is usable, especially if it's free.

QUICK TIPS (SIZE AND SALES) ~

You must think outside the box when it comes to couponing. You may get a $1.00 off coupon for "Showeet Cereal". You notice the Showeet Cereal is not on sale this week. Now instead of trying to use the coupon for a box of Showeet Cereal, maybe you can purchase a single cup of Showeet Cereal? Read the coupon and make sure it doesn't indicate or have size restrictions. Let's say Showeet Cereal in a cup is $1.00 and your manufacturer's coupon is for $1.00. Now the coupon covers the entire cost of Showeet Cereal. Another tip is the "travel section." Some coupons do not indicate size. When that is the case, take those coupons and use them on travel size items; but only if they cover at least 90% of the cost. You will obtain a lot of coupons in the weekly circulars; your job is to find deals with them.

Only use coupons on sale items. For instance, you have a buy one get one free coupon; you think that a great deal because you're getting one free. I say wait until the store says if you buy one free they will give you one free. Purchase two at a time and give one coupon. Now you have a free item from the store, and a free item from the manufacturer. If you can't find any deals on the coupons, hold them because a lot of stores will wait until the last minute to have sales on items that have coupons.

Another sweet spot that exists inside of every grocery store is the clearance section/ scratch and dent section. You are allowed to use coupons on these items as well. If you cannot use the coupon and they are expired, donate the coupons to the military. They are allowed to use coupons after they have expired. Check with your grocery store also, because a few will take expired coupons. The address to mail expired coupons to the military will be in the back of this book.

Now it may seem like a waste, to only use 45% or less of the coupons that come in the inserts. Do not feel obligated to use all the coupons because you purchased them. Let me tell you now you will not use most of them and it's ok.

WHERE TO GET COUPONS ~

I know you want to know where one gets coupons. I will give you that information here. Free places for coupons are:

redplum.com

smartsource.com

coupons.com

Pgeveryday.com

These are just a few, you must go online and to your research, there are many more. Many manufacturers will give you coupons themselves; check their website. These sites will allow you to print two per computer/ device. It is illegal to make copies of what your printed. The coupons printed have serial number on them that are tracked though the company's website. Many times these sites will only give out a certain number so you must get the coupons while they are available.

The internet coupons are a great tool if you have a printer. I would suggest going to these sites above and doing your homework to find more. If you do not have a printer, visit your local library to print what you need. Most couponers purchase the coupons directly from the Sunday paper. Sunday's newspaper comes with a packet that contains upcoming store's weekly ads and inserts. Inserts included are the Red Plum (RP), Smart Source (SS) and PG (Proctor & Gamble) this last one comes out once a month.

Coupon inserts are not given during the week of any Federal holiday. Go to Washingtonpost.com to obtain one free insert. They will ask you to fill out a form with your name and address it will be mailed on Thursday morning. It may take a week or two for delivery to begin. You can also speak with your mailman/woman to see if they have any extra inserts. If so, ask them to give them to you. They deliver them on Tuesday where I live. You can check with your local paper; some local papers include inserts (Red Plum, and Smart Source) Coupon inserts are free.

Google "clipping services". This is a tool for those who want to bypass clipping. You pay a fee to the clipper and they will mail you coupons you select. There is a fee and it something like $1.50 for 10 of the same coupon. Now just like any other site, be careful when buying. There are a lot of scammers online that just want to take your money. I also suggest using PayPal; never give out your bank information to a stranger. Once you find someone you trust I suggest sticking with them.

COUPON BUDDIES ~

Now that you know where to get coupons let me give you some good advice. Find you a coupon buddy, and work as a team. I speak with my coupon buddy every morning and we tell each other which deals we are going for the day. This helps the both you maximize your savings.

If you're married or dating your spouse or dating partner may not want to talk coupons with you. This was something I had to learn the hard way. My husband told me all that I seem to talk about lately was coupons. He was right, I was so excited about the daily deals I wanted him to know about each and every one of them. To my disappointment he wasn't interested. That's funny to me since he does partake of everything in this house, but I learned to discuss coupons with my coupon buddy which allows me to get out that pinned up excitement. Plus, couponing is really only exciting to those who coupon. I learned that along the way.

More advice; Share, share, share your coupons with each other. My coupon buddy and I share all the time. We don't eat many carbohydrates in my home, so if I obtain rice, pasta or white grains she already knows she can have them. My family only eats one type of mayonnaise her family doesn't really care for mayonnaise. If she gets the mayonnaise coupons and I need some, I already know they are mine. The more coupon buddies you have the bigger your team gets and the more savings you will all find. Work together and take over in the coupon community. Once a month get together and host a clip and taste. Have a pot luck style dinner and clip coupons together? Trust me this is a fun activity and it makes clipping coupons fun. At this pot luck share deals, strengths weaknesses and help each other overcome.

> **NOTE:**
> One thing a couponer never shares is their home-base store. This is the store where they find everything they have coupons for. Keep that information to yourself, if you share that information with the wrong person and one day you'll regret it.

COUPONING VS GROCERY SHOPPING ~

Couponing and shopping are two separate things. I never shop for groceries on coupon days. Stores have so many other great deals but you must stay focused on the task at hand. Tell yourself, "I am only here to get the items I have coupons for". I coupon Monday thru Thursday. You must have discipline to only get what you have coupons for. The grocery stores' main agenda is to get you to purchase other items. Stores are in business to make a profit. Stay committed to only get what you have come to get. Grocery shopping usually occurs for me on Friday. I do not coupon on weekends.

When I grocery shop I get items that I cannot get with coupons which are fresh produce, and fresh meat. Find a local farm or farmers market to purchase your fresh produce. If the farmer can sell directly to you, the consumer, they have cut out the middle man, "the grocery store." The prices should be lower; always check before your purchase. Also note; do not purchase produce that's not in season. If they store carries the item they will charge you more for a non-seasoned item. Every meat department places sale stickers on meat three days before the expiration date. If you can, ask the meat department which day they place those yellow stickers on the meat. If they can't disclose that information, you check the date on the meat and come back three days before they expire. These coupons do not double and meat can last in a deep freezer up to 3-6 months.

You should only use coupons on sale items. Even if you have the extra money, still remember to only use coupons on sale items to maximize your savings. Your grocery budget and your coupon budget are not the same. Make an extra budget for couponing. Included in this budget should be the price for newspapers, ink and printing paper if you plan on using the internet printable (IP) coupons, as well as items you are purchasing for the month with coupons. Stay in your budget to maximize savings. You must have the willpower to stay within your "pre-planned" budget.

I remember one of my first stockpile item. Which was also my first freebie? It was ice cream bars. I had so much ice cream I needed an ice cream truck. Now what was I going to do with all that ice cream? First of all, I didn't even have the space to hold all that ice cream. I was so excited to use coupons I wasn't thinking about where I would put my first haul. I went online and read where someone said take the ice cream bars out of the box and put them in Ziploc bags to save space. I thank GOD for that post. I had no space for real food. So every cookout and party I was invited to I brought ice cream. I was so happy to get rid of that ice cream. Looking back at it now, I'm sure people thought I was thoughtful. Not the case at all. I wanted to get rid of that ice cream so bad I had needed to make space for other things like real food. Lesson here: Only purchase what you have space to hold. Only purchase what you will use. Unless you can donate it to an organization or church, don't buy the item. Many items will spoil so look for the expiration date on the box before you make a large purchase. You may want to invest in another freezer or refrigerator. I just wanted to put that in your mind now so that you can prepare.

ORGANIZING ~

Organization is key you must keep your coupons organized or you may miss out on a deal. All coupons expire; you must pay attention to the expiration date. I am a visual person so the way I organize may not work for you. Do what works for you. I like to see my coupons laid out. I have a large table where they are precut and paper clipped together in a neat pile. I revisit these piles of coupons at least once a day. Some couponers like to keep the coupons in the insert until they see a sale to use them. In very small print along the perforation of the insert you will see the month, day and year the insert came out.

Many couponers keep their coupons in a file folder according to the date it was printed. When they need a coupon out of the insert they go to a website called southernsavers.com. This website is a coupon database and it will give you the exact date a coupon was issued and which insert it was found in. It will also let you know if the coupon you're looking for is a printable.

I like to already have them cut and ready to go. This process is totally up to you. Most couponers have their big ole coupon binder in the shopping cart. I have a couple of accordion folders I choose to keep at home. I take my coupons that I am using and place them in a white envelope. I may have 10 envelopes in my purse because I already know many items I will purchase before I go into the store and I have already calculated my out of pocket (OOP) cost. I write the product, the amount and total on the outside of the envelope.

In my opinion it is smart to go in a store incognito just in case you have to make one purchase go to your car and repeat. No one can tell that you are a couponer, especially if you don't look or have items like coupons binders with you. Some couponers complain that they are followed in stores. Well if they didn't make it so obvious no one would be able to tell. It's not illegal to coupon, so why should you care if someone is following you anyway. I have never run into issues like these, but then again I go in with a plan and execute it quickly. I grab exactly what I have coupons for and leave. I've seen people in store with inserts walking and cutting at the same time. To each his own, so do what works for you.

I have to re-emphasize that in order to have success in couponing you should only use your coupons on sale items. This is how you maximize on your savings. Once you have purchased your Sunday paper, open the plastic bag and go over each stores' sales. Then match up your coupons with the sales in the sales paper. Grab a note book and write down the item's sales price and subtract your coupon amount. You goal is to save.

KEEP IT LOW ~

When couponing, I do not to go over $1.00 for items listed below. Yes, many of these listed items you can get for free. This takes time, proper planning and diligence in couponing. The only thing I really ever pay $1.00 for is laundry detergent and bleach. You have to figure out what your cut off price is for stock piling. Most couponers choose not to go over

50 cents when they are stockpiling (purchasing more than normal) Do what works for you.

*Personal care items:☐

Shampoo
Conditioner ☐
Body Wash
Bar soap☐
Shave Cream☐
Disposable Razors☐
Refillable Razors☐
Deodorant☐
Toothbrush
Toothpaste
Floss ☐
Lotion☐
Face Items☐
Feminine Products

* House hold items:☐

Toilet Paper☐
Paper Towels☐
Laundry Detergent
Fabric Softener☐
Dryer Sheets☐
Dish Soap☐
Cleaning Sprays☐
Air Fresheners☐
Storage Bags

☐ * Food items:☐

Snacks☐
Juice
Water
Bacon☐
Coffee☐
Canned Food☐
Frozen Food☐
Condiments
Hot Dogs, Sausages
Lunch Meat
Spices
Sugar

When most people start couponing, they think it has a lot to do with food. In my opinion it's 30 percent food, 40 Personal care items,☐20 percent house hold items, 10 percent pet food/treat items. It's completely up to you as to how you go about going after these percentages. I suggest you don't waste your time chasing every deal, all deals are not good deals.

For instance, I currently have over 100 bottles of body wash. Body wash will be on sale every week and I'm almost certain there will be coupons for body wash. The only deal I will chase on body wash is if I can find it for pennies, nickels, or dimes. I will always get items when they are close to free. If I don't have space, I will donate the items. I suggest you do the same, find a church, homeless shelter, or woman's shelter or give it to a family you know that may be in need. Do well with what you have, your stock pile will grow so much you won't have enough room for it all. Good comes back when you do well.

When you start couponing it's a little hard to determine whether you have a good deal or not. Well you've got to ask yourself now much would you normally pay for that product? If it's close to what you would normally pay and you have a coupon, that's not a good deal. Your coupon should cover at least 50% of the cost before you make a purchase.

PLAN AND PACE YOURSELF ~

Couponing can be over whelming at times. When it or if it becomes over whelming, take a break. You are the CEO of couponing in your household. There will always be sale, deals and freebies. Some couponers coupon full time for six months, then take a break for six months. They fill up their house, they chase every deal and pack up with everything their family will need for the next six months. For me I have to admit I have never gone off of couponing over a week at a time. I still purchase my inserts from the weekly paper during my off week, but I may not feel like, cutting, or looking for deals so I don't. Some coupons expire quickly and some come with a long expiration date. Either way take a break when you need one. The coupon business of your home can't survive if the CEO doesn't take care of his/ her self. You get in what you put in with coupons.

I look at it like a part time job and handle myself accordingly. I coupon for about 4 hours a day 5 days a week. Not four hours straight, it's divided up throughout the course of my day. Most of my cutting and planning is done at night while the baby is sleep. The day time is really when I execute what I have planned the night before.

I am a stay at home mom with one hubby, three girls and two pit bulls. My mornings are hectic getting my older girls out the house and off to school as well as my handsome husband. During the day I have my 14 month old with me who I call my little coupon buddy. My little coupon buddy will only tolerate a certain amount of shopping. It's very important for me to get in and out especially if we have more than one store to go to on that particular day. If you're a stay at home parent I suggest you purchase a crock pot and start dinner before you leave the house, especially if your family is accustomed to a home-cooked meal like mine. Crock pot meals save time and allow you to focus on couponing and putting your haul away. Some mornings I start a load of laundry and when I return that load goes in the dryer. Multi-tasking is how I get many things done. If you're a stay at home parent, I suggest finding effective ways multi-task. It's so much to get done in the window of daylight. When my girls walk in the door, we discuss their day and I assist with homework if needed.

The best time to coupon is totally depends on where you live and if you live in a high couponing area, like me. If so you should never wait to purchase any items that you can get free with coupons. This should always be top priority with you. You have to think like this; you're not the only person who wants freebies and most of the times the early bird gets the worm. In the coupon world the bird who get there first takes all the worms. Don't judge the persons or people who take it all.

Most couponers donate to homeless shelters, and many other places that are in need. If you're a stay at home parent you have an advantage. Most people shop after work. If you work, I suggest going before work on all freebies. Or go on Sunday as soon as you get your newspapers clip them right away. Some couponers like to go to the stores when they are busy and some prefer to go when they are slow. It really doesn't matter what time you go just choose a time that you feel comfortable with. I find that men have more confidence at couponing than women. Now don't get upset with me ladies it's just something that I have observed. Men are just more confident and they are great at getting the job done. For some reason or another some women get nervous when it comes to couponing? Maybe because it new to them I'm not really sure, either way your must has confidence when your coupon. I know for a fact that cashiers read people well. If you're unsure they will double check every coupon making it more stressful on the person who lacks confidence. If this is you fake, it till you make it. Put on your best confidence face. Talk with the cashier ask them how they are doing, etc. It's great to make friend at the stores where you frequently shop. Cashiers know things like when they store may put items on clearance, and when stores may have special events like super doubles. Make small talk to avoid jitters if you're nervous. Its ok coupons are not illegal stores welcome coupons. The more you do it the less nervous you'll become.

GROCERY STORE POLICIES ~

Below is a list of some of the more popular grocery store coupon policies. If your local grocery store is not listed below, ask your store about their coupon policies.

Most grocery stores double up to 99 cents; meaning if the coupon is 75 cents, it will double to $1.50. However, most grocery stores do not give overage; meaning if the item is for $1.49, your 75 cents coupon will be auto adjusted to $1.49. Below is the list of some stores' doubling policies.

➢ **Dollar General** – Does not double coupons – 4 duplicate coupons per transaction. Make multiple transactions to maximize your savings.

- ➢ **Dollar Tree** – Does not double coupons – 4 duplicate coupons per transaction, do multiple transactions
- ➢ **Giant** – Doubles up to 99 cents; only 4 duplicate coupons will double. After the 4th, system will deduct coupon at face value. For example, if you have five .50/1 chips coupons, only 4 of it will double to $1 and the last one is valued at 50 cents. To maximize your savings, do multiple transactions.
- ➢ **Shop Rite** – Doubles $1.00 coupons to $2.00, however, you must spend $25.00 at the end of the transaction (after all coupons have been scanned.) They will only scan 4 duplicate coupons and 20 coupons a day per card.
- ➢ **Safeway** – no limits coupons up to .99 cents will double
- ➢ **Target** – Does not double coupons – 4 of the same coupon per transaction.⍰
- ➢ **Family Dollar** – Does not double coupons – 4 duplicate coupons per transaction, do multiple transactions.
- ➢ **Rite Aid** – Does not double coupons.
- ➢ **Harris Teeter** – Same as Giant and only 3 duplicate internet printable (IP) will double. Only 20 coupons per day, per card, will double.
- ➢ **Walgreen's** – Does not double coupons –
- ➢ **Weis** – Same as Giant and they do allow overage; but will not give you money back. So if your coupon value is higher than the price item, grab a filler. What is a filler you ask? An item to get you out of overage; many grab a stick of gum a bag of chips or an item they really need.⍰

COUPON MATH ~

(How it doubles if you shop at a store that doubles up to .99 cents)

.20=.40

.30=.60

.40=.80

.50=1.00

.55=1.10

.60=1.20

.70=1.40

.75=1.50

.80=1.60

.90=1.80

.95=1.90

Super double Events (same as above however they will also double 1.00 & 2.00 coupons) during super double most couponers focus on higher value coupons.

1.00=2.00

1.50=3.00

2.00=4.00

CVS ~

NOTE: Coupons at CVS (coupons do not double)

CVS is known for their Redbox located inside of every CVS. The Redbox offers in store coupons and percentage off coupons, which can be stacked with manufacture coupons. Percentage off coupons from the Redbox cannot be used on sale items. The Redbox also offers freebies. I check that Redbox every Monday. I live 2 miles away from CVS. New coupons can be printed once a week. CVS is also known for extra cash bucks (Ecb) as well as extra beauty bucks (ebb). ⬚Coupons do not double at CVS. Couponers must sign up for an extra care card in order to receive the sales prices at CVS. If you do not have one, go to any cashier and fill out the form and you will receive one instantly.

Your card will give you access to the red box as well as your extra care buck (Ecb) and Extra beauty bucks (Ebb) will be track on your extra care card. I recommend you register your card online for extra savings like percentages off your total order. These type of coupons may be stacked with store coupons, manufacture coupons, and Redbox coupons. Here at CVS you can stack coupons from the red box with Extra Care Bucks (Ecb) you may have earned from a previous purchase along with your manufacture coupons. This is how you maximize on your savings. Here is an example below:

> Showeet Paper Towels $5.99
> Manufacturer's coupon 2.00
> CVS sales offer: Spend $30.00 and receive
> $10.00 Extra Care Bucks (Ecb)
> 5 x 5.99=29.95
> 5x 2.00 = 10 .00 Total 19.95

You pay $19.95 and after you complete your order the cashier will give you $10.00 extra care bucks (Ecb) on a future purchase, which you can use right away. If you have more coupons do the deal above again.

Next order:

Showeet paper towels $5.99

Manufacturer coupon $2.00

CVS sales offer: Spend $30.00 and receive $10.00 Extra Care Bucks (Ecb)

Math

$5.99x5 = $29.95

$2.00 x 5=$10.00

Extra Care Bucks (Ecb) from 1st transaction $10.00

Total cost after coupons and Ecb = 9.95

When this transaction is complete, the cashier will hand you another 10.00 Extra Care Bucks (Ecb).

This example above this is what couponers call rolling = doing the same deal over and over. You must pay attention to the sales paper. Some offers are limit one, some are not.

Most Couponers at CVS only use the previous extra care bucks (Ecb) on other offers that give extra care bucks (Ecb's), which means you must do the homework. Look at the sales paper, see which offers are offering Ecb so you can use a previous Ecb to lower your out of pocket (OOP) cost. Pair this with manufacturer coupons or/and store coupons. If you cannot find another deal to roll your previous extra care bucks (Ecb) its ok; just make sure you redeem your extra care bucks (Ecb) before it expires on items that you can pair with store coupons and/or manufacturer coupons.

Store Coupon Policy

Information located at www.cvs.com

Digital reproductions of offers shall not be accepted (such as using a mobile application to reproduce an image of an offer/coupon).CVS/pharmacy Coupon Policy CVS/pharmacy coupons (ExtraBucks® Rewards and ExtraCare® Coupons) and Third Party Manufacturer Coupons are accepted in our retail stores in accordance with the following guidelines: CVS/pharmacy does not accept expired coupons. CVS/pharmacy will not accept third party manufacturers' coupons with another retailer's logo Coupons cannot be exchanged for cash or gift cards. Third Party Manufacturer coupons are issued by a third party and sales tax may be charged on pre-coupon price. CVS/pharmacy does not accept coupons for items not carried in our stores. CVS/pharmacy only accepts ExtraBucks Rewards applicable to the ExtraCare card offered at time of purchase. CVS/pharmacy does not currently accept coupon bar code images displayed on a Smartphone, iPhone, Droid etc. The total value of the coupons may not exceed the value of the transaction. Sales tax must be paid, if required by state law. Certain CVS/pharmacy coupons may be subject to state sales tax rules similar to Third Party Manufacturer Coupons and sales tax may be charged on pre-coupon price Language at the bottom of CVS/pharmacy coupons provides specific coupon acceptance rules. Any coupon offers not covered in these guidelines may be accepted at the discretion of CVS management. Sale Items CVS/pharmacy will accept manufacturer coupons for an item that is on sale. CVS/pharmacy will not accept percent off coupons for an item that is on sale. In the event that any item's price is less than the value of the coupon, CVS/pharmacy will only accept the coupon only to the price of the item. CVS/pharmacy does not provide cash back in exchange for any coupons. Multiple Coupons CVS/pharmacy accepts one manufacturer coupon and applicable CVS/pharmacy coupon(s) per item, unless prohibited by either coupon offer. There is no limit to the number of ExtraBucks Rewards that may be used in a transaction as long as it does not exceed the transaction total. The number of manufacturer coupons used in a transaction may not exceed the number of items in the transaction. The coupon amount will be reduced if it exceeds the value of the item after other discounts or coupons are applied. (For example, a $5.00 coupon for a $4.99 item will result in a $4.99 coupon value). CVS/pharmacy accepts multiple identical coupons for multiple qualifying items as long as there is sufficient stock to satisfy other customers, unless a limit is specified. Management reserves the right to limit the quantity of items purchased.

CVS/pharmacy reserves the right to process coupons in any order. CVS/pharmacy accepts multiple Dollar off Transaction coupons (e.g. $3 off $15) in one transaction if they apply To Ex. Customer may use two 3 off $15 coupons if they are purchasing over $30.00 Buy One, Get One Free Coupons Sales tax must be paid for any Buy One, Get One Free coupon offer, if required by applicable state laws. Two coupons may be used on a Buy One, Get One Free promotion as long as it does not exceed the item total o Ex. Suave Shampoo is on sale for $2.00 Buy One, Get One Free and the customer is purchasing two shampoos; customer may use two coupons for $1.00 each and pay the applicable tax. Buy One, Get One Free promotions may be combined with Buy One, Get One Free Coupons. Customers are responsible for paying applicable tax o Ex. Suave Shampoo is on sale for $2.00 BOGO and customer has a MFG coupon for Suave BOGO. Customer will receive both items for free but will need to pay any applicable tax. Internet/Print at Home Coupons CVS/pharmacy accepts internet/print at home coupons that include a barcode. CVS/pharmacy will not accept reproductions or rebates

WALGREENS ~

NOTE: Coupons at Walgreens (Coupons do not double)

Walgreen's is known for register rewards. Coupons do not double here at Walgreen's they are taken at face value. Walgreen's is also known for stacking store coupons with manufacture coupons. Store coupons at Walgreen's are given out monthly and go fast. Please check with your local Walgreen's and ask what date the new one will they be available. You also need a Walgreen's rewards card if you do not already have one please go to a cashier to obtain one. You will need a card for sale price items and a place to load your points. Once you receive your card register your card online. Walgreen's is also known for their point system. Certain items mostly sale items also come with points the more points you obtain the more spendable money you can use at Walgreen's this is all tracked on your Walgreen's card.

This is the point system in a nut shell

5,000 points = $5.00

10,000 points = $10.00

18,000 points = $20.00

30,000 points =$35.00

40,000 points = $50.00

You may redeem points anytime, just tell the cashier that you are using your points to pay for your total.

Walgreens will not accept an internet printable for a free item that does not require a purchase. Walgreen's does not allow overage, and will not accept a coupon that exceeds the selling price of an item. Walgreen's Register Rewards earned for deals are limit 1 (if multiple transactions are allowed, do it in order to take advantage of the register rewards) if not go back every day until the deal is over to maximize on the register rewards.▢

➢ Register Rewards are usually coupons for a certain amount off your bill for a future purchase. You will receive your register rewards after your transaction is finished. The cashier will hand you a paper coupon printed from the register. Now if you feel you should have received one at the end of a purchase talk with the cashier before you leave the store. They can go over the transaction with you or get a manager for further assistance
➢ Couponers who shop at Walgreen's go for sale items attached with points to maximize their savings. Most shoppers shop here for points even if they don't need the item. (Donate)
➢ Walgreens will not allow you to use coupons that exceed sale price. If you have a coupon for $2.99 and the item cost $3.00 Walgreens will not sale you the item.

Here's an example below using a store coupon and manufacturers coupon:

Showeet Candy on sale for $2.75 plus 1000 points

Manufacturer coupon on Showeet Candy $1.00
Store Coupon .75 cent
Purchase 1 Showeet Candy $2.75
Use 1 store coupon
Use 1 manufacture coupon
Math
$2.75- $1.00-.75=$1.00
Your Out of Pocket (OOP) cost
$1.00 plus you received 1,000 points

Repeat process until all of your coupons are finished. Depending on your Walgreens, you may have to do one transaction at a time. Store coupons states limit one. If they allow you to spilt the transaction great. If not come back tomorrow or drive to another Walgreens. Remember slow and steady wins the race.

Store Coupon Policy

Walgreens Coupon Policyholders General Guidelines www.Walgreens.com

1. All coupons are to be presented to the cashier at the time of checkout.
2. Walgreens does not accept expired coupons. Coupons expire at 11:59 p.m. on the expiration date at the point of sale, whether in store or online.
3. Walgreens will not accept fraudulent or counterfeit coupons as determined by Walgreens.
4. Unless otherwise specified, all coupons have no cash value. Coupons and their face value cannot be exchanged for cash or gift cards.
5. Competitor's coupons shall not be accepted by Walgreens.
6. The number of manufacturer coupons, including Register Rewards®/Savings Rewards manufacturer coupons, shall not exceed the number of items in the transaction. The total value of the coupons shall not exceed the value of the transaction. Sales tax must be paid, if required by state law.
7. Walgreens will not accept coupons that exceed the selling price of an item and no cash back is ever provided in exchange for any coupons.
8. Coupons that appear distorted, blurry or altered in any way shall not be accepted; all coupons must have a clear and scannable bar code.
9. For offers when multiple items are purchased and additional items are free (buy 1 get 1 free; buy 2 get 1 free, etc.), the number of coupons applied to that offer cannot exceed the number of items required in the "buy" portion of the offer.
10. Coupons may not be applied against any free item received in any offer (See 7 above).

11. Paper coupons will be processed before digital coupons.
12. Walgreens shall not accept coupons for items not carried in our stores.
13. Walgreens reserves the right to limit quantities to customers and employees.
14. Manufacturer coupons must include a valid redemption address.
15. Coupons may be subject to advertised offer limitations and all other limitations and restrictions on the applicable coupon or product.
16. Walgreens shall accept manufacturer coupons for items that are on sale.

The General Guidelines apply to the categories below and are to be referenced in addition to the specific coupon category guidelines.

Multiple Coupons

The guidelines below are to be followed in addition to the General Guidelines listed above.

1. When purchasing a single item, Walgreens accepts one manufacturer coupon and applicable Walgreens coupon(s) for the purchase of a single item, unless prohibited by either coupon offer.
2. When purchasing multiple items, Walgreens accepts multiple coupons for multiple qualifying items, as long as there is sufficient stock to satisfy other customers, unless a limit is specified on the coupon. Management reserves the right to limit the quantity of items purchased and/or prohibit the purchase of excessive quantities. An excessive quantity is any quantity above and beyond normal household usage.

Buy 1 Get 1 Free Coupons

The guidelines below are to be followed in addition to the General Guidelines listed above.

When items are featured in a Buy 1 Get 1 Free promotion, at least one product needs to be purchased. A maximum of one BOGO coupon is permitted per two qualifying items in a BOGO offer.

Internet Printed Coupons

``The guidelines below are to be followed in addition to the General Guidelines listed above.

Walgreens shall not accept "free product" internet printed coupons.

Register Rewards®/Savings Rewards coupons

The guidelines below are to be followed in addition to the General Guidelines listed above.

Earning Register Rewards®/Savings Rewards

1. Register Rewards/Savings Rewards will only print for in-stock merchandise during the promotional period.
2. Register Rewards/Savings Rewards can only be earned for eligible items. No substitutions are permitted.
3. There is a limit of one Register Rewards/Savings Rewards coupon per offer per customer per transaction.
4. Customers redeeming a Register Rewards/Savings Rewards against the same offer may not receive another Register Rewards/Savings Rewards coupon.

Redeeming Register Rewards®/Savings Rewards

Customers redeeming a Register Rewards/Savings coupon against the same offer shall not receive another Register Rewards/Savings Rewards coupon.

1. The number of manufacturer coupons, including Register Rewards/Savings Rewards manufacturer coupons, shall not exceed the number of items in the transaction.
2. Register Rewards/Savings Rewards shall be forfeited if the qualifying merchandise is returned.
3. Register Rewards/Savings Rewards can be redeemed for eligible items only. Ineligible items include but are not limited to:
   - Alcoholic beverages
   - Dairy products
   - Gift cards/phone cards/general purpose reloadable cards
   - Health care services, including immunizations
   - Lottery tickets
   - Money orders/transfers
   - Postage stamps
   - Prescription Savings Club membership fee
   - Prescriptions
   - Special event/entertainment tickets or passes
   - Tobacco products
   - Transportation passes

∘Any items prohibited by law

Digital/Paperless Coupons

The guidelines below are to be followed in addition to the General Guidelines listed above. Only digital coupons, attached to your Walgreens Balance® Rewards account, shall be honored. Digital reproductions of offers shall not be accepted (such as using a mobile application to reproduce an image of an offer/coupon).

WEIS ~

NOTE: Coupons at Weis (Coupons double up to .99)

Weis is known for sale prices on meat in the meat department. They have buy one get one free on meat and percentage off meat. Coupons up to .99 cents will double at Weis. They will only take 4 duplicate coupons in each transaction. Weis will only take one coupon for each item. In order to receive sale price, you must obtain a Weis card. If you do not have a Weis card, please go to customer service provide your driver's license and receive one immediately. Weis will not accept "free product" internet printed manufacturer coupons. Weis will accept "bogo" internet printed manufacture coupons. Weis Market will accept internet coupons up to a $10.00 limit. Weis will not give cash back, so do not let your transaction fall below zero. Always grab a filler dollar item like gum or mints. I normally grab a $1.00 dish soap for a filler that is my number one item I purchase as a filler.

Showeet Cereal 1.75

Manufacturer coupon on Showeet cereal .75 cent
Purchase 4 Showeet Cereal at $1.75 each
Use 4 Showeet Cereal coupons at .75 each
$1.75 x 4 = $7.00
.75 + .75 = 1.50 coupons under .99 cents will double at Weis
$1.50 x 4=$6.00
Your Out of Pocket (OOP) cost
$7.00 - $6.00 = $1.00 on 4 boxes of Showeet Cereal

If you have more coupons for Showeet cereal repeat the above process until you are out of coupons. The only coupon limitation at Weis you may only do 4 duplicate coupons per transaction. Which means you must divide your transaction into 4 each time.

Weis Coupon Policy www.weismarket.com

Manufacturer and Store Coupons:

1. Coupons are redeemable only by a customer purchasing the specific brands and product(s) stated on the coupon, with the face value of the coupon deducted from the retail or club card price.
2. Coupons must be for products sold at Weis Markets and coupons must be presented at the time of the transaction.
3. Coupons are subject to advertised offer limitations and all other limitations and restrictions on coupon.
4. Coupons cannot be applied against the item received in any offer where a customer buys one or more items to get one or more items free.
5. Coupons amount may be reduced so that any combined discounts and coupons do not exceed the value of the item.
6. Coupons have no cash value.
7. Accepted coupons must be manufacturer or Weis Markets store issued coupons for specific items only.
8. Weis Markets will accept valid manufacturer coupons that display another retailer's logo or name only if such coupon is for a specific item.
9. Weis Markets will accept valid Catalina manufacturer coupon that is issued to a customer by another retailer only if such coupon is for a specific item.
10. The coupons must have an expiration date.
11. Coupons are void if they appear distorted or blurry, are altered in any way or copied.
12. The transaction amount may not fall below zero value, or go negative, meaning we will not give the customer money back.
13. All sales taxes are paid by the customer at the full value of the item.
14. All bottle deposits on the purchased and free items are paid by the customer.

15. Weis Markets reserves the right to refuse any coupons at its discretion.
16. Only four (4) coupons will be accepted on four (4) of the same product per household per day.

Internet Printed Coupons:

17. Weis Markets gladly accepts internet printed coupons. The same manufacturer and store coupon rules above apply to all internet printed coupons.
18. Internet printed coupons must scan at the registers.
19. Internet printed coupons must have serial numbers and follow an industry- standard format.
20. Manufacturer internet printed coupons must clearly indicate that they are a manufacturer coupon and have a valid manufacture address on the printed coupon.
21. Weis Markets will not accept "Free Product" Internet printed Manufacturer coupons.
22. Weis Markets will accept "BOGO" Internet printed Manufacturer coupons.
23. Weis Markets will accept internet coupons up to a $10.00 limit.
24. Check with the local store regarding "Double Coupon" advertised promotions where customers will receive double the coupons face value off the regular or club card price up to the advertised limit. Not all locations offer double coupon promotions. Limitations and restrictions for double coupon promotions may change at any time. Changes will be posted in the store. Please see your local stores for details.
25. Weis Markets does not allow a customer to redeem two or more manufactures coupons against the same item in a single transaction.
26. If a customer presents two coupons for the same item in a single transaction, Weis Markets will only accept the first coupon to be applied in the system.
27. Weis Markets will double up to four of the same alike coupons as long as the customer purchased the items to go along with the coupons.

TARGET ~

NOTE: Coupons at Target (Coupons do not double at Target)

Target is known for their cartwheel app, as well as store coupons (found on target.com) which they allow you stack with a manufacture coupon. Target is also known to give out gift cards for purchasing some of their pre-selected items. You can also price match at Target with their listed competitors which you may find on their website. When you are price matching at Target you can use your cell phone to match the prices of anyone they have on the competitors list. Once you have found a lower price target will honor the price you have found. Then you can use your coupons to lower your out of pocket (OOP) cost. You can only use four like coupons per transaction. If you have more than four coupons, you must split up your order in fours.

Example:

> Purchase 4 Showeet candles and receive a five-dollar gift card.
> 4 Showeet candles $2.99
> You have a $.50 Showeet candle coupon from Target
> You have a $1.50 manufacture coupon from the newspaper
> Math
> $2.99 x 4=$11.96
> $.50 x4=$2.00
> $1.50X4=$6.00
> 11.96-2.00-6.00=3.96

You pay 3.96 when you finish the transaction the cashier will give you a $5.00 gift card. So essential they paid you to take those four candles home. I know you had to come out of your pocket but they gave it back plus 1.04. Most couponers would take that five-dollar gift card and do the above transaction again. In the second transaction you wouldn't have spent anything. Now if your Target won't allow a second transaction you have seven days to come back and repeat the above scenario. When you do this in the coupon world we call it "rolling" doing the same transaction over and over until you've run out of coupons.

Store Coupon Policy
Target Stores Coupon Policy www.target.com

Coupons are a great way to save even more when shopping with us, and it's easy to use them at our stores. When accepting coupons, we follow the guidelines below to ensure all guests have the opportunity to purchase products at great prices.

Manufacturer and Target Coupons:

•Only one manufacturer coupon (paper or Cartwheel digital), one Target coupon (mobile or paper), and one Cartwheel℠ offer can be combined per item (unless otherwise noted on coupon).

•We have the right to refuse, or limit the use of any coupon and/or the subsequent return for any reason, including if guests' reoccurring behavior becomes disruptive or the items are deemed not to be for the purpose of using or gifting.

•Limit of 4 identical coupons per household, per day (unless otherwise noted on coupon).

•We do not accept expired coupons.

•All valid coupons must be presented to the cashier during checkout and have a scannable barcode.

•Item purchased must match the coupon description (brand, size, quantity, color, flavor, etc.). Acceptance of unmatched coupons is against policy.

•Coupons are void if copied, scanned, transferred, purchased, sold, prohibited by law, or altered.

•Coupon amount may be reduced if it exceeds the value of the item after other discounts or coupons are applied.

•We do not give cash back if the face value of a coupon is greater than the purchase value of the item.

•Guest pays tax on full retail value, including the coupon value, of Manufacturer Coupons. Target coupons reduce the taxable value.

•We cannot accept coupons from other retailers, or coupons for products not carried in our stores.

•Some items may not be available at all stores.

•We regularly monitor the Coupon Information Corporation (CIC) website for counterfeit coupons. We do not accept counterfeit coupons.

•Our Quantity Limit Policy is available on the policy board near Guest Services. We reserve the right to limit quantities. Note that the Quantity Limit Policy is in place for all transactions regardless of coupon usage.

Internet (Print-at-Home) Coupons:

•We gladly accept valid internet coupons with a scannable barcode.

•We do not accept internet coupons for free items with no purchase requirements.

Category/Department and Storewide Coupons:

•If redeeming more than one category/department or storewide coupon, you must meet the purchase requirements for each coupon individually.

•Percent off coupons including Category Coupons, will apply to all qualifying items in the transaction. No other same category/department or storewide coupon will apply.

Buy One Get One Free Coupons (BOGO):

•BOGO coupons cannot be combined (i.e. you cannot use two BOGO coupons on two items and get both for free). Unless stated otherwise on the coupon, the use of one Buy One Get One Free coupon requires that two of the valid items are presented at checkout of which one item will be charged to the guest and the 2nd item will be discounted by its full retail price.

•A second cents-off coupon of the same type cannot be redeemed towards the purchase price of the first item.

•If a Target BOGO coupon is used, one additional manufacturer coupon may be used on the first item.

•If a Manufacturer BOGO coupon is used, one additional Target coupon may be used on the first item.

RITE AID ~

NOTE: Coupons at Rite Aid (Coupons do not double)

Rite Aid is known for their Plenti point system. The Plenti programs includes an array of companies like AT&T, Exxon, Macy's, Mobil, and Rite Aid. Go to plenti.com to learn more. Earn Plenti points on things you buy every day at Plenti partners; some of your favorite supermarkets, and hundreds of online retailers. Plenti points are rewards earned and used with Plenti partners. Members of wellness+ with Plenti can earn Plenti points when they make eligible purchases at Rite Aid and other Plenti partners.

What Rite Aid currently calls +UP Rewards have transitioned to Plenti points. Plenti points give you even more ways to save and customers have at least two years to use them. Plenti points can be used the next day on another purchase. The points are tracked though your card and the telephone number you give them when you filled out the application. To maximize your savings, try to only use coupons on items that also have Plenti points. You must have $2.00 worth of Plenti points accumulated before your first use. Plenti points obtained in a transaction will be available to use the next business day after 6 a.m.

Example:

Showeet Lipstick $4.00

Manufacturers coupon on Showeet Lip Stick $3.00

Purchase 4 Showeet Lip Stick $4.00 each

Use 4 Showeet Lip Stick Coupons $3.00 each

$4.00 x 4=$16.00

$3.00 x 4=$12.00

Your Out of Pocket (OOP) cost

$16.00- $12.00=$4.00 on 4 Showeet Lip Stick

If you have more coupons repeat steps above until you are out of coupons. If the policy is a maximum of four of the same coupon and the store will not sell you any more, return the next day or drive to another Rite Aid and repeat steps above.

Store Coupon Policy
Rite Aid www.riteaid.com Rite Aid Coupon Acceptance Policy

At Rite Aid, we gladly accept many coupon types—including manufacturer coupons found in newspapers and magazines, as well as print-at-home coupons—to ensure you get the most value for your dollar. We accept the following coupon types as detailed in the coupon acceptance guidelines listed below:

COUPON TYPES:

Manufacturer Coupons - Manufacturer coupons are found in newspapers, magazines and even affixed to products. The UPC on these coupons begins with a "5."

Rite Aid Manufacturer Coupons - Rite Aid Manufacturer coupons generally appear in our weekly circular, on our website and are sent to customers via email. These coupons are labeled "manufacturer coupon" and have a UPC that begins with "49."

Rite Aid Valuable Coupons - Rite Aid coupons are labeled "Valuable Coupon" and have a UPC that begins with "48."

Internet/Print at Home coupons - Rite Aid will accept internet / print at home coupons.

Ecoupons - Rite Aid and its business partners make electronic coupons available that can be loaded directly on a wellness+ card or Plenti card. The register automatically "rings" the coupon when the qualifying item is scanned. Ecoupons are subject to the same rules as other coupons as defined in this policy.

Buy One, Get One Free - Rite Aid accepts Buy One, Get One Free coupons, however only one coupon can be used for each pair of items purchased.⬛ A customer can use one "cents off" coupon (a coupon of fixed value such as $.50, $1.25, etc.) in conjunction with the item they are purchasing on a Buy One, Get One Free promotion (or with a Buy One, Get One Free coupon), although the value of the cents off coupon cannot exceed the selling price of the item.⬛ Customers can use up to two coupons with a Buy One, Get One at a % off promotion, provided the total value of the coupons does not exceed the selling price of the two items combined.⬛

Buy One, Get One Free coupons cannot be used in conjunction with a Buy One, Get One Free or with a Buy One, Get One at a % off promotion.

Total Purchase Coupons - Rite Aid may feature total purchase coupons, which discount the total purchase amount based upon meeting specific requirements.⬛ For example, $5 off a $25 purchase price threshold coupon.⬛ These coupons are accepted under the following conditions:⬛

- The coupon is valid and in date; only one total purchase coupon per transaction.
- Total purchase equals or exceeds $25 before tax (before any coupons are applied).
- Coupons for individual items can also be used including another "48" coupon that is tied to an item in the transaction.
- Provided the total of items purchased is equal to or greater than the purchase requirement, other coupons can be used in conjunction with the total purchase coupon.

ACCEPTANCE GUIDELINES:

General Guidelines:

- Coupons must be valid and in date; Coupons cannot be exchanged for cash.⬛
- Register will validate coupon through scanning or keyed entry of the coupon UPC number.⬛⬛
- In the event that any item's selling price is less than the value of the coupon, Rite Aid will accept the coupon in exchange for the selling price of the item.⬛ Coupon redemption can never exceed the selling price of an item and no cash back is allowed.

- When making a return for a product that had a coupon attached, Rite Aid cannot refund cash for the value of the coupon and cannot return the coupon that was used.⯀⯀
- Rite Aid reserves the right to not accept any coupon where the validity or the coupon cannot be established.
- Multiple Coupons:
- More than one coupon can be used on the purchase of a single item under the following conditions:⯀
- All coupons match the item being purchased.
- The total of the coupons is equal to or less than the selling price of the item before sales tax.
- No more than one "48" Rite Aid Valuable coupon, one "49" Rite Aid Manufacturer coupon, and one "5" Manufacturer coupon can be used on a single item. Rite Aid may accept up to 4 identical coupons for the same number of qualifying items as long as there is sufficient stock to satisfy other customers within the store manager's sole discretion.

SHOPRITE ~

NOTE: Coupons at ShopRite (Coupons double up to 1.00 if you spend $25)

ShopRite is known for having Ecoupons attached to the ShopRite Card. If you do not have a ShopRite Card, you can obtain one from customer service and you will need to show them your driver's license. They will give you one right away. Once you have your card, I suggest going online to register your card through their website. ShopRite will allow you to stack the Ecoupons loaded onto your card with manufacturer coupons. Use this to your benefit.

ShopRite will double 20 coupons per day; this information is tracked on your Shop Rite savings card. Once you have reached 20, it will only take the rest at face value. In those 20 coupons, only 4 may be the same. Essentially you may only take home 4 chips, 4 sodas, 4 teas, 4 waters, and 4 ice cream sandwiches; or you can purchase 20 waters in five separate transactions. Shop Rite is also known for doubling $1.00 coupons. I would highly recommend using his to your advantage. I would only use $1.00 coupons at this store and the register will deduct $2.00 per coupon; this is amazing! However, in order to take advantage of this amazing double you must spend $25.00. This requires strategic planning on your end because this means that your total has to be $ 25.00 after your 20 coupons have been applied.

Example:

Manufacture Coupon $1.00

Showeet coffee creamers

Item price = $2.00

$1.00 Coupon x4 =4.00 in Coupons that will double to 8.00 if you spend $25.00

Out of Pocket cost 0.00 on Showeet coffee creamer

Remember $1.00 coupons always double here unless is specifies "do not double on the coupon"

Store Coupon Policy
Information located at www.shoprite.com

At ShopRite®, we know that coupons are an important tool to help you save money. That's why it's our goal to make using coupons at ShopRite® stores easy for our customers. We welcome all ShopRite®-issued coupons along with valid manufacturer-issued coupons, valid Internet coupons and valid electronic coupons loaded on your Price Plus® club card.

ShopRite® stores redeem coupons in accordance with manufacturer guidelines and the terms printed on the coupons. To help ensure product availability and an efficient checkout experience for all customers, the use of excessive amounts of coupons or multiple identical coupons may be limited at the store manager's discretion. When redeeming coupons at ShopRite® stores, please be sure to:

1. Present your coupons at the time of purchase. ShopRite from Home® customers must present coupons when picking up an order or at the time of delivery. We cannot give cash back or credit for coupons not presented at time of purchase.
2. Present your Price Plus® club card to the cashier. Your card is required to redeem any digital coupons you may have loaded to your Price Plus® club card at shoprite.com. If you do not have your Price Plus® club card, you may access it by using the phone number on record in your Price Plus® club card profile. Customers who have downloaded the ShopRite mobile app may use the digital Price Plus® club card feature in the app. The ShopRite mobile app is the ONLY app we will accept at the checkout in place of your Price Plus® club card.
3. Redeem your coupons within the time period printed on the coupon. We do not accept expired coupons.
4. Match your purchase to the specific item indicated on the coupon. No substitutions are permitted on manufacturer-issued coupons.
5. Use manufacturer-issued Internet coupons that are legible with a valid remit address and a bar code that scans. Internet coupons that

have been identified as counterfeit do not scan in our system and will not be accepted. We reserve the right to refuse any coupon for "free" product, "buy one get one free" offers, and those with a high value in relationship to the item's price.

6. Note your store's current double coupon policy. Double coupon policies vary by store. Check your store for details. We will double up to four identical coupons per household per day unless further restricted by the manufacturer.

7. Additional coupon restrictions are listed below:

8. We reserve the right to limit coupon redemptions to four (4) of the same coupon per household per day.

9. Unless expressly prohibited by the terms on the coupon, we accept checkout (Catalina) coupons and manufacturer-issued coupons that display other retailer logos only if they are clearly identified as manufacturer coupons and if they scan at checkout.

10. We do not accept coupons that have been identified as counterfeit and reserve the right to refuse any coupon that appears to be fraudulent. Coupons displaying signs of mass cutting or similar cuts and tears, coupons bearing tape, coupons in mint condition, and coupons bearing sequential numbers may suggest coupon fraud.

11. If the coupon's face value or multiplied value is greater than the purchase price of the item, the item will be free. We will not give cash back or apply additional credit.

12. Only one manufacturer coupon will be applied to each "Buy One, Get One Free" offer.

13. We cannot refund the value of a coupon or return the coupon if a purchased item is later returned to the store.

14. Customers must pay any and all applicable taxes. The cash value of any ShopRite®-issued coupon is 1/100¢.

15. ShopRite® stores do not accept coupons or savings offers presented in the form of a bar code on a mobile phone or other mobile electronic device.

16. Coupons are non-transferable, and may not be copied, photocopied, scanned, altered, sold, traded, or otherwise distributed to others. Coupons that are copied, photocopied, scanned, altered, sold, traded, distributed or transferred by their original recipient to any other person, firm or group are VOID.

17. This Coupon policy may be modified at the store manager's discretion and is subject to change.

MEIJER ~

NOTE: Coupons at Meijer (do not double)

Meijer is known for having big savings that come from the mPerks program, which features eCoupons, personalized deals and monthly choices of various rewards when you make select purchases. Some locations accept competitor coupons and allow stacking of store and manufacturer coupons. You will have to ask your local Meijer if they allow coupon stacking (more than one coupon on an item) Log in to your MPerks account to load digital coupons. Remember, MPerks digital manufacturer coupons may not be combined with a paper manufacturer coupon on the same item. You can only do this is if the MPerks coupon is labeled "Store Coupon" or "Meijer Coupon." In that case, you may use both the digital coupon and a manufacturer coupon on the same item.

Example:

Sweet Showeet Dipping Sauce, $1.69

Manufacturer Coupon $1.00

Math

$1.69-$1.00 =$ 0.69

Store Coupon Policy
Information located at www.meijer.com
What is the Meijer store Coupon Acceptance policy?
Published 10/25/2010 01:35 PM | Updated 08/21/2015 03:12 PM
Accepted coupon types include: Meijer, manufacturer, Catalina (Meijer and manufacturer), mPerks, and competitor coupons within certain guidelines:
• Coupons must be presented on or before the expiration date.
• All coupon terms and conditions must be met and validated by the checkout register.

- Customers may use one manufacturer coupon (paper or digital) per item.
- Customers may also combine one manufacturer coupon per item with applicable Meijer coupon(s) where allowed under coupon redemption terms.
- In the event one manufacturer digital coupon is attempted together with one manufacturer paper coupon toward the purchase of the same item, the checkout register will prompt you to choose which to apply. The coupon not applied will be returned to you.
- Digital coupon acceptance is limited to mPerks only. Digital coupons from smartphone apps will not be accepted.
- Transactions cannot be broken up to avoid coupon stacking restrictions.
- Separate check lanes will not be opened or designated for customers with large coupon orders.
- Manufacturer coupons and Catalina manufacturer coupons require the customer to pay sales tax on the full retail amount.
- Meijer, Catalina Meijer, and competitor coupons require the customer to pay sales tax only on the discounted item price.
- Meijer will accept competitor coupons from Food Retailers or Mass Merchandise Retailers.
- Meijer defines Mass Merchandise Retailers as a retail store offering both food and general merchandise/apparel under one roof. Coupons from Club Stores and Dollar Stores will not be accepted.
- Meijer does not accept competitor coupons for beer, wine, liquor, cigarettes, double or triple coupons, clearance, percent off, total transaction discounts, special promotions, gift card promotions, limited quantity items, mail-in rebate offers, and going out of business sales.
- If the value of a coupon is more than the price of the item after discounts or other coupons have been applied, the value of the coupon will be applied up to the reduced price of the item.
- Meijer does not apply the excess value of a coupon to the order total if the value of the coupon is over the price of the item after other discounts or coupons are applied.
- Meijer reserves the right to limit coupon quantities and to determine the order of application of multiple coupons and/or promotions.

SAFEWAY ~

NOTE: Coupons at Safeway (Coupons double up to .99)

Safeway is known for Just4u extra savings that they apply directly to your Safeway Card. You must register your card online. Once you register your Safeway Card the website or app allows you to click on items you want to have extra savings on. I normally click them all, just in case I get a manufacturer coupon which I can stack with for extra savings. Safeway is also known for not having a limit on how many coupons you may use in one transaction. Many couponers enjoy going to Safeway because of this reason alone.

Example:

You have one hundred 75 cents coupons for Showeet Water

Showeet Water cost $1.99 a pack so $1.99 multiplied by 100 equals $199.00

Take one hundred of your Showeet Water items as well as your one hundred Showeet Water coupons to your cashier.

Your total before your coupons would be $199.00; total after coupons $49.00

Now I know you're asking yourself why I would ever spend $49.00 on water this month. Well, would you ever be able to get 100 six packs of water at a lower price? If the answer is no, then this is a steal and one piece of your stockpile puzzle. Once this purchase is made you can move on to the next piece of your puzzle. Safeway is also known for having great $5.00 specials on Friday. Check your local Safeway to see what they have to offer.

Manufacture Coupon .75 cent

Store Price $ 1.99

Math .75 plus .75 = $1.50

1.99- 1.50 = .49 cent per six pack

Before coupon $1.99 x 100= $199.00

After Coupon .49 x 100= $49.00

This is how you should calculate your out of pocket (OOP) cost on every item you purchase. Grab a note book and do the math. You should always know how much your total cost will be. Somtimes I have had to cancel my order or do the order again. The registers are not always correct. One reason it could be incorrect is the price on the item may not be in the system correct. Or it can be an error on the cashier's part; maybe they didn't ring up all of the coupons handed to them? Remember you're the pro at this so do your homework before you leave home.

Store Coupon Policy
Safeway Coupon Acceptance Policy www.safeway.com
This policy applies to Safeway Inc. and its affiliates and subsidiaries in the USA

Manufacturer and Store Coupons:

1. We will redeem coupons only for the specific items included in our customer's purchase transaction. The redemption value will be as stated on the coupon, unless that value yields a final price for such item less than zero; if application of the redemption value yields a price less than zero, the coupon will be redeemed only for the amount that yields a zero price (our customer cannot net a cash credit or payout from a coupon purchase).
2. Paper coupons must be presented at the time of the purchase transaction. We will accept only coupons issued by Safeway or the manufacturer of the relevant product. We will not accept photocopies of coupons.
3. Coupons are subject to advertised offer limitations and all other limitations and restrictions on the applicable coupon or product.

4. Coupons may not be applied against any free item received in any offer.

5. Coupons have no cash value.

6. Safeway will not accept manufacturer coupons (including, but not limited to, coupons issued through a Catalina or other in-store coupon dispenser) that display another retailer's logo or name unless such coupon is for a specific item with the same product identifiers as the product included in our customer's purchase transaction and is sold and available at the store.

7. We will not accept coupons unless they have an expiration date. Expired coupons will not be accepted.

8. We will not accept coupons that, in the determination of Safeway personnel, appear distorted or blurry or are altered in any way.

9. Sales taxes will be applied in accordance with the law of the applicable state, regardless of any coupon or other discount that may apply to the purchase transaction.

10. All applicable bottle and packaging deposits on the purchased and free items must be paid by the customer.

11. Safeway reserves the right to refuse any coupons at its discretion.

12. Purchase reward thresholds (if any) will be calculated based upon customer's final price (after deducting Club Card savings and all other discounts and savings) before deductions for any manufacturer coupons. As an example (and not as an offer), if a $10 minimum purchase is required for a customer reward, a customer's order at full retail would be $12, a Club Card discount of $1.75 applies, and a manufacturer's coupon of $1 applies, the customer would be given credit for a $10.25 purchase, and would be eligible for the reward (assuming compliance with all other requirements) even though the customer's cash payment would be only $9.25. The manufacturer's coupon would not be deducted from the total for purposes of determining reward eligibility. Purchase reward thresholds (if any) will be calculated based upon customer's final price (after deducting Club Card savings, and all other discounts)

13. References to a threshold purchase requirement will exclude purchases of: Beer, Wine, Spirits, Tobacco Products, Fuel, All Fluid Items in the Refrigerated Dairy Section (including Fluid Dairy and Dairy Substitutes), Prescription Items and Co-payments, Bus/Commuter Passes, Fishing/Hunting Licenses and Tags, Postage Stamps, Money Orders, Money Transfers, Ski Tickets, Amusement Park Tickets, Event Tickets, Lottery Tickets, Phone Cards, Gift Cards,

and Gift Certificates; also excluded are: Bottle Deposits, Redemption Values, and Sales Taxes.

Internet Printed Coupons:

14. We accept internet printed coupons. The same manufacturer and store coupon rules above apply to all internet printed coupons.
15. Internet printed coupons must be capable of scanning at checkout.
16. Internet printed coupons must have serial numbers and must follow an industry-standard format.
17. Manufacturer internet printed coupons must clearly indicate that they are a manufacturer coupon and must have a valid manufacture address on the printed coupon.
18. We will not accept "free product" internet printed manufacturer coupons.

Load to Card Club Coupons:

19. Internet and digital coupons that have been electronically loaded to a Safeway Club Card are automatically redeemed at the time of purchase after the club card number has been entered. All other coupon policies above apply to electronic coupons that are loaded to a club card. Internet and digital coupons electronically loaded to a Safeway Club Card are not included in any operative "double coupon" or other increase in coupon value promotion. Coupons are not accepted on online shopping orders made on Safeway.com, except Internet and digital coupons that have been electronically loaded the 'Safeway Club Card' being used for that order.

Doubling of Coupons:

20. Check with your local store regarding "double coupon" promotions where customers will receive double the manufacturer coupon face value off the regular or club card price up to the identified limit. Not all locations offer double coupon promotions and the terms of such promotions may differ by time and store. Limitations and restrictions for double coupon promotions may change at any time. Changes will be posted in store only. "Double coupon" promotions do not apply to any internet or digital coupons except for applicable internet printed manufacturer coupons. These explanations and restrictions on "double coupons" apply to any promotion that increases the value of a manufacturer coupon beyond its face value.

Coupon Stacking:

21. Safeway does not allow a customer to redeem two or more manufacturer coupons against the same item in a single transaction.

22. Coupon stacking policies for manufacturer coupons apply to paper and electronic coupons that have been loaded to a club card.

23. If a customer presents two coupons for the same item in a single transaction, Safeway will give the highest discount for that item, subject to the terms of the applicable offer and/or coupon.

Rainchecks:

24. Rainchecks are for one time use only.

25. Rainchecks expire ninety (90) days from the date issued and will be accepted at any Safeway store that has the specific item in stock.

26. We reserve the right to limit Raincheck quantities based on product availability and advertised limits.

27. Rainchecks can be issued for up to six (6) items unless otherwise stated in the applicable advertisement.

28. Rainchecks will not be issued for Beer, Wine, Spirits, Tobacco Products, Fuel, All Fluid Items in the Refrigerated Dairy Section (including Fluid Dairy and Dairy Substitutes).

29. Rainchecks can be offered for store super coupon items unless otherwise specified on the coupon. Rainchecks will not be provided for items advertised as "clearance", "while supplies last," "limited quantities," or other designation indicating a limited supply.

All coupon redemption terms are subject to our Coupon Acceptance Policy in effect at time of redemption.

We may change the terms of our Coupon Acceptance Policy at any time. Such changes may become effective without advance notice or advertisement. The current Coupon Acceptance Policy will be posted at the customer service area in each store. You are also advised to periodically check our website for any changes to the terms of our Coupon Acceptance Policy.

WALMART ~

NOTE: Coupons at Walmart (coupons do not double here)

Walmart is known for price matching and their app called "savings catcher." When price matching at Walmart you can use your cell phone/ or current store add to show the lowest price found and they will honor the competitors' lowest price. The saving catcher app searches for lower prices for the items you have purchased. If the app finds your items at a lower price they will give you your items at that price. The extra money that you have already spent at Walmart will be returned on your Walmart account. You will set up an account once you download the app. For further information regarding the saving catcher please go to Walmart.com. Walmart is the only store in my area that allows overage from coupons.

Example:

If you have a Showeet Toothpaste coupons for $1.00 and Walmart has Showeet Toothpaste on sale for 0.95 cent. The cashier will hand you 0.05 at the end of your transaction.

Purchase 10 Showeet Toothpaste for $0.95
Use 10 Showeet Manufacture Coupons for $1.00
Math
$0.95x 10=$9.5
$1.00 x 10 = $10.00

Two things can happen here; the cashier can give you your change. Or the overage can be applied on another item in your order. The decision is completely yours.

Store Coupon Policy

Walmart Coupon Policy www.corporate.walmart.com

We gladly accept the following types of coupons*

- Print-at-home internet coupons
- Must be legible
- Must have "Manufacturer Coupon" printed on them
- Must have a valid remit address for the manufacturer
- Must have a valid expiration date
- Must have a scannable bar code
- Buy one, get one free (BOGO) coupons with a specified price
- Are acceptable in black and white or color
- May not be duplicated
- Manufacturers' coupons
- For dollar/cents off
- We honor the manufacturer limitations
- For free items (except those printed off the Internet)
- Buy one, get one free (BOGO) coupons
- Must have "Manufacturer Coupon" printed on them
- Must have a valid remit address for the manufacturer
- Must have a valid expiration date
- Must have a scannable bar code
- May not be duplicated
- Competitors' coupons
- A specific item for a specified price, for example, $2.99
- Buy one get one free (BOGO) coupons for items with a specified price
- Have a valid expiration date
- Are acceptable in black & white or color
- May not be duplicated
- Soft drink container caps
- Checkout coupons ("Catalina's")
- Printed at our competitors' registers for dollar/cents off on a specific item
- Must have "Manufacturer Coupon" with specific item requirements printed on them
- Must have a valid remit address for the manufacturer
- Must have a valid expiration date
- Must have a scan able bar code
- Are acceptable in black & white or color
- May not be duplicated

We do not accept the following coupons:

- Checkout coupons

- Dollars/cents or percentage off the entire basket purchase
- Print-at-home Internet coupons that require no purchase
- Competitors' coupons
- Dollars/cents off at a specific retailer
- Percentage off
- Buy one, get one free (BOGO) coupons without a specified price
- Double- or triple-value coupons

*The following are guidelines and limitations:

- We only accept coupons for merchandise that we sell.
- Coupons must be presented at the time of purchase.
- Only one coupon per item.
- We have the ability to limit the number of identical coupons and the number of coupons for the same item per transaction.
- Item purchased must be identical to the coupon (size, quantity, brand, flavor, color, etc.).
- Coupons must have an expiration date and be presented within the valid dates.
- If coupon value exceeds the price of the item, the excess may be given to the customer as cash or applied toward the basket purchase.
- In all situations, we reserve the right to limit purchase quantities to typical retail purchase quantities or one-per-customer or household and to exclude dealers.
- Store Managers have the final decision in taking care of the customer.
- SNAP items purchased in a SNAP transaction are ineligible for cash back.
- WIC items purchased in a WIC transaction are applied to the basket purchase and may not be eligible for cash back. Refer to state-specific WIC guidelines.
- The system will prompt for supervisor verification for:
- 4 or more like coupons per transaction.
- A coupon of $5 and over.
- $50 or more in coupons in one transaction.
- Coupons totaling a percentage (%) off of the total sale.

DOLLAR TREE ~

NOTE: Coupons at Dollar Tree (coupons do not double here)

This is the secret spot; most items end up here towards the end of a sale cycle. Items like shampoo, conditioner, aspirin, drinks, cake mix, candy, lip balm, and some frozen foods. Coupons do not double in value here. If you have a 50 cent coupon that is all that will be deducted from your total. At Dollar Tree, you are only allowed to use 4 duplicate coupons in a transaction. Example one you have 20 coupons for a brand-named soap and more for $1.00. The Dollar Tree will only allow 4 coupons per transaction. Which means your grab 4 soaps and more you have your 4 coupons in hand. You allow the cashier to ring you up. You total is $4.20 the cashier scans your coupon for $1.00 off four times. Your final total will be .20 cent I added state tax. Each state has different tax. Now you have 16 coupons left for the product soap and more. You can either get 4 more to do the transaction again. Now this depends on the management at your local Dollar Tree. Some will allow a repeat transaction and some will not. They have the right to say, "No, we only honor four duplicate coupons a day." Now if you run into that, you know from here on out to bring some extra family members each time you have more than 4 duplicate coupons. If you have patience; which you will need to have in the coupon business, go back tomorrow and get 4 more. Repeat the process until all your coupons have been used. Never let freebies go to waste. I know it maybe an inconvenience to go back tomorrow, but slow and steady wins the race.

Example:

Manufacturer Coupon $1.00

Item Cost $1.00

Math

$1.00 - $1.00 = 0$

Out of pocket (OOP) will be tax only.

You will always be responsible for state tax, so when you know you have free items always take a change purse/bag. One tip: You can always leave a zip lock bag of change in your glove compartment. I get excited when I just have to spend pennies, nickels and dimes. Sometimes I do a little dance at the register; a victory dance is what I like to call it.

Store Coupon Policy

Dollar Tree Coupon Acceptance Policy ww.dollartree.com
Manufacturer Coupons

•We accept Manufacturer Coupons only. We do not accept retail-specific coupons, such as those of Target, Wal-Mart, etc.

•We do not accept photocopies of coupons. Coupons must be intact and not altered or modified in any way.

•Coupons can only be used in stores, must be presented at time of purchase, and cannot be redeemed for cash at a later time.

•Item purchased must match the coupon description (brand, size, quantity, color, etc.) and be presented prior to the expiration date printed on the coupon.

•We accept only one (1) Manufacturer Coupon per single item purchased

•We accept coupons for over a dollar on a single item, but the coupon value will be reduced to the purchase price of the item.

•We cannot give cash back if the face value of a coupon is greater than the purchase price of the item.

- We accept coupons for over a dollar on multiple items if the coupon amount does not exceed the combined retail price of the items indicated.

- We accept up to four (4) like coupons per household per day.

- Coupons for free items are only accepted if a purchase is required to get one free (for example, Buy One Get One Free offers).

- Any applicable sales tax must be paid by consumer.

- We reserve the right to accept, refuse, or limit the use of any coupon.

- This policy is subject to all local, state, and federal laws and regulations where applicable.

- These guidelines apply to all coupons accepted at Dollar Tree (Manufacturer and Internet Coupons).

Internet Coupons

- We accept up to two (2) Internet Coupons per household per day.

- Internet Coupons must be a "Manufacturer Coupon", have a valid expiration date, and must have a valid remit address for the manufacturer.

- We do not accept Internet Coupons for "Free" items with no purchase requirements.

- Duplicated (photocopies) Internet Coupons will not be accepted. Each Internet Coupon must have a different serial number.

Last Revision: July 28, 2014

FAMILY DOLLAR ~

NOTE: Coupons at Family Dollar (do not double)

Family Dollar is known for ad matching (you must have the paper ad in hand) and stacking store coupons with manufacturer coupons. Use stacking coupons to your advantage. Family dollar is also known for having decent prices on many items. Coupons do not double here. All coupons will be taken at face value. You must go into the store and get a circular for the store coupons that are attached inside. Most in-store coupons at Family Dollar say limit one per customer. This is where your family members come in handy. Bring them with you to do multiple transactions. If you don't have anyone available to join while shopping at Family Dollar, shop there daily to obtain the savings for stacking store coupons with manufacturer coupons. Some stores will allow you to do separate transactions and some will not; it depends on management. When you are price matching another store you are also allowed to use in-store coupons and manufacture coupons on the sale item. Take advantage of the price matching at Family Dollar.

Example:

> You have a Wal-Mart Ad that says a Showeet Coffee on sale for $2.99
>
> Take the Ad in the store with you.
>
> You see that Family Dollars in-store Ad has a 50 cents coupon for Showeet Coffee
>
> You have a 75 cents manufacturer coupon for Showeet Coffee

Take all three to the cash register plus the Showeet Coffee they have for $4.99

$2.99-.50-.75=$1.74

Since coupons do not double at Family Dollar, your final price is $1.74.

Store Coupon Policy
Information located at www.familydollar.com
Family Dollar Stores ACCEPT Manufacturer and Family Dollar issued coupons including:

•Printed Coupons
•Internet Coupons
•Mobile Coupons

Family Dollar Stores ACCEPT Manufacturer and Family Dollar issued coupons that meet these requirements:

◦Only ONE Manufacturer coupon and ONE Family Dollar coupon can be used per ITEM in a transaction.▯
◦Duplicate coupons in one transaction are accepted as long as there is an item purchased for each coupon.
◦All Family Dollar coupons must have a scan able barcode or valid promotion code.
◦Printed coupons must be original (no photocopies) and have a printed expiration date.
◦Internet coupons may either be in black and white or color and must be legible and read "Family Dollar" or "Manufacturer Coupon".
◦Mobile coupons must have a valid promotion code.

Please note:

•Coupons can be redeemed only for items that are described on the coupon. The copy on the coupon dictates which items are to be included in the offer, not the image of what is shown on the coupon.
•Coupons can be redeemed if the value of the coupon is greater than the price of the item. In this case, the value of the coupon will be discounted to match the price of the item.▯
•Family Dollar $5 off $25 coupon is accepted as long as the net purchase, AFTER all other offers, coupons and/or discounts have been applied is $25 or more.
•Coupons are acceptable for use on sale or clearance items.

Family Dollar does NOT ACCEPT coupons that:

- Are from other retailers.
- Are expired.
- Are in home (internet) printed "Free Item" coupons that do not require a purchase.⁂
- Are manufacturer coupons that do not have a "remit to" address on the coupon.
- Are bottle caps.

Please note:
- Competitor coupons are not matched.
- Screen shots or photos of printed coupons are not accepted

Dollar Tree www.dollartree.com

The subscription for text messages is a recurring service. You will receive recurring text messages. Message & data rates may apply. Send STOP to cancel.

Text HELP for info or contact mobiletexts@dollartree.com. Send STOP to cancel the service.

You must have a two-way text-enabled phone with compatible carrier and plan.

You may consent to receive text messages from Dollar Tree. Text messages may contain advertisements. These messages will be generated by automatic telephone dialing systems. Consent not required to be eligible to purchase products from Dollar Tree.

You must have a two-way text-enabled phone with compatible carrier and plan. Compatible carriers include AT&T, Sprint, T-MobileÂ®, Verizon Wireless, Alltel Wireless, Boost Mobile, Cricket Communications/Leap Wireless, MetroPCS, U.S. CellularÂ®, Virgin Mobile USA, Aio Wireless, Alaska Communications Systems Wireless (ACS), All West Wireless, BlueGrass Cellular, C Spire Wireless, Carolina West Wireless, Cellcom, Cellular One of East Central Illinois (ECIT), Cellular One of Montana (MTPCS), Chariton Valley Cellular, Chat Mobility, Cincinnati Bell, Cross Communications, CTC Telecom, DTC Wireless/Advantage Wireless Systems, Duet IP, Eagle Telephone Systems/Snake River PCS, East Kentucky Network/Appalachian Wireless (EKN), Element Mobile, Epic PCS, Farmers Mutual Telephone Company (FMTC), GCI Wireless, Golden State Cellular, Goldstar Communications/Silverstar PCS, I Wireless (Iowa Wireless), Illinois Valley Cellular, Immix/Keystone Wireless, Inland Cellular, Manti Tele Communications Company/Breakaway Wireless, Mobi PCS, MobileNation/SI Wireless, Mosaic Telecom, MTA Wireless/Matanuska Kenai, Nex-Tech Wireless, Northwest Missouri Cellular, nTelos, Nucla-Naturita Telephone Company/NNTC Wireless, Panhandle Wireless (PTCI), Peoples Wireless, Pine Cellular, Pioneer

Cellular, Plateau Wireless, Revol Wireless, Simmetry Wireless, South Central Communications, SouthernLINC Wireless, SRT Wireless/North Dakota Network, Strata Networks/UBET Wireless, Thumb Cellular, Union Wireless, United Wireless, Viaero Wireless & West Central Wireless (WCC).

GIANT ~

NOTE: Coupons at Giant (coupons double up to .99)

Giant is known for gas points. You must take advantage of this perk at Giant. In order to do so you must first have a Giant bonus card. I suggest you go online and register your card, they have just started to give extra benefits to people who have registered their cards online. In order to take advantage of this, look through their sales paper for items you can pair with manufacturer coupons. You want to lower your OOP cost so that you can redeem your points at the gas station. Now every sale at Giant will not have gas points attached to them. You must examine the sales paper from week to week. Every once in a while you can matchup coupons with a sale item from the gas point list. When you cannot match coupons with gas point items you still may want to purchase these items to lower your price on gas. The choice is yours.

How it works

www.giantfoods.com information obtained directly from Giant's website

Save 10¢ per gallon for every 100 points you earn. You earn 1 point for every dollar you spend with your Giant Card. Points are valid for 30 days.

100 points = 10¢/gallon

200 points = 20¢/gallon

300 points = 30¢/gallon

...up to $2.20/gallon!

Here is an example below:

Showeet Soup at $1.75 plus 50 gas points on each soup

Manufacturer coupon on Showeet Soup .75 cent

Purchase 4 Showeet Soup at $1.75 each

Use 4 Showeet Soup coupons at .75 each

$1.75 x 4 = $7.00

.75 + .75 = 1.50 coupons under .99 cents will double at Giant

$1.50 x 4=$6.00

Your Out of Pocket (OOP) cost:

$7.00-$6.00 = $1.00 on 4 cans of Showeet Soup

50 x 4=200 gas points

200 gas points = .20 off of your gas purchase

If you have more coupons do this deal as many times as you can. The gas points will continue to add up onto your bonus card. At Giant you are only allowed to use 4 duplicate coupons in each transaction. Split your transaction up, and don't worry, your gas points are accumulated and tracked on your bonus card. You have thirty days to use your gas points, don't let them expire.

Store Policy

Store Policy Giant Food (East Coast) www.giantfood.com Coupon Policy
•Only 1 manufacturer's coupon may be redeemed per item; No substitutions are allowed.⏎
•The exact item stated on the coupon be must be purchased in order to redeem the coupon.
•Coupons cannot be redeemed after the expiration date stated on the coupon.⏎
•The total redemption value of the coupon may not exceed the retail value of the item purchased.
•Any coupons for "free" products will be honored for the value of the item only. "Free" coupons cannot be doubled or tripled.

•Smart source coupons cannot be doubled or tripled.

•Product specific Checkout Coupons cannot be doubled or tripled.

•Product specific Checkout Coupons cannot be used with any other manufacturers' coupons for the same item.

•Non-product specific store Checkout Coupons can be used with another manufacturers' coupon. For example: a customer may use a coupon for "50¢ off any Produce item" and a manufacturers' coupon on the same item.

Double coupon policy

•We double the savings marked on manufacturers' cents-off coupons up to 99¢. Any coupon $1 and over will be redeemed at face value of the item purchased. In cases where the double coupon total exceeds the value of the item, the offer is limited to the retail price. Lottery tickets, cigarettes, tax and items prohibited by law are excluded.

•You may double a maximum of 4 identical manufacturers' coupons. For example: if a customer purchased five boxes of Cheerios and presented 5 manufacturers' coupons for 50¢, the first four coupons would be doubled to $1. The fifth coupon would only be redeemed for 50¢.

•Up to an additional 12 identical manufacturers' coupons/items will be redeemed at face value for a total of 16 identical manufacturers' coupons.

Competitor's coupons:

•Giant will accept competitor's coupons for products, provided the customer has met the purchase requirements as stated on the face of the coupon. We do not honor manufacturer's coupons that state that they are only redeemable at a specific retailer. Also, if a competitor coupon is for an item that does not indicate a size, we will only match it for an item size that both Giant and the competitor carry. We do not honor point promotions or continuity programs.

Internet Coupons

•We do accept Internet coupons unless we are notified of fraudulent activity involving specific Internet coupons.

Coupons on gift card purchases:

•Giant Food does not accept coupons of any type for the purchase of gift cards.

*We reserve the right to limit quantities.

HARRIS TEETER ~

NOTE: Coupons at Harris Teeter (Coupons Double up to .99)

Harris Teeter is known for their Super Double Events (they occur 4 times or more a year) please check with your local Harris Teeter for super double events. You must have an e-VIC card to receive sale prices. If you need to obtain an e-VIC card, you can do so at customer service. They will need to see a current driver's license and you will get an e-VIC card instantly.

Harris Teeter is also known for their family meal deal, please check your local Harris Teeter to take part of this amazing offer. Harris Teeter will double 20 coupons a day with a face value of .99 cents and below. Harris Teeter limits 3 like coupons which is tracked by your e-VIC card. After you have reached 20 that day, the rest of your coupons will be taken at face value. Ecoupons offered through Harris Teeter once you register your card online may be stacked with manufacturer coupons. Use the Ecoupons to your advantage and always look for manufacturer coupons to match the store's Ecoupon to lower your out of pocket (OOP) cost.

Buy one get one free items ring up half price for each item; which means you can purchase only one if you like. When you see buy two get three free you must purchase all five to receive discounts on suggested items. Side note: Harris Teeter has amazing sales on eggs; always check the dairy department when shopping.

I want to go into depth here in reference to Super Doubles at Harris Teeter. This event is a big one in coupon world. Couponers plan in advance. Here is the best advice:

1. Familiarize yourself with the store before your first Super Double. Walk up and down each aisle and familiarize yourself with what is in each aisle. The more you shop at Harris Teeter you will begin to know where everything is located so you won't waste time on locating deals.
2. Only use your $1.00 and $2.00 coupons during this time. The $1.00 coupon will double to $2.00 and the $2.00 coupon will double to $4.00.
3. Get there early as most couponers will have already been inside of the 24 hour Harris Teeters. Even though the registers begin sales at 7:00 a.m., couponers would have arrived by 5-6 am and shopped for an hour or two to be ready to check out at 7:00 a.m.
4. Get rain checks on items that have already been sold out. The early bird really gets the worm on this one during Super Doubles because it is first come first served.
5. Be sure to be patient and extra nice to your cashier; realizing this is a hectic time for them.
6. Have your coupons in order and ready to give to the cashier before you get in is or their line. Your transaction should always be a smooth one on your part.

Example:

>Manufacturer coupon on Showeet Cheese 75 cents
>
>Purchase 4 Showeet Cheese at $1.75 each
>
>Use 3 Showeet Cheese coupons at .75 cents each
>
>$1.75 x 3=$5.25
>
>$0.75 + $0.75 = $1.50 coupons under .99 cents will double at Harris Teeter
>
>$1.50 x 3=$4.50
>
>Your Out of Pocket (OOP) cost

$5.25 - 4.50 = $0.75 on 3 Showeet Cheese

Harris Teeter Super Double

Manufacturer coupon on Showeet Pizza $2.00

Purchase 3 Showeet Pizza at $4.00 each

Use 3 Showeet Pizza coupons at $2.00 each

$4.00 x 3=$12.00

During Super Doubles $2.00 and under will double $2.00 + $ 2.00 = $4.00

$4.00 x 3=$12.00

Your Out of Pocket (OOP) cost

0.00 + State Tax

You are only allowed to use 3 like coupons at Harris Teeter per transaction. Harris Teeter will only double 20 coupons per day. This information is tracked on your E-VIC card. If you have more coupons for cheese and you want to do this deal again you must divide your transaction up in threes; they will only take 3 like coupons. If you have other coupons, you want to use you must factor in that they will only double 20 per day. However, you can use as many coupons as you like.

- Coupons presented and items purchased must match exactly; size, variety, flavor, etc.
- We uphold any purchase stipulations set forth by product manufacturer.
- We accept only one paper coupon (Manufacturer, Internet, Harris Teeter or Competitor) per purchased item.
- Coupons saved to mobile devices cannot be accepted.
- We accept coupons for items only of equal or more value; we do not give cash back.
- Sales tax is paid by customer at full retail.
- We do not accept photo copied coupons of any type.

Doubling

- We accept 20 double coupons per day per customer/household with VIC card; all others redeemed at face value. No orders may be separated that would allow the 20 coupon limit or any other coupon limits to be exceeded.
- We double manufacturer's coupons up to face value of $.99; with total amount not to exceed $1.98 or entire retail of item; whichever is less.
- We double up to three identical items with manufacturer coupon; additional coupons for like item will be honored at face value. Like items include all flavors.
- No competitor coupons will be doubled or tripled.
- Coupons that state "do not double" will not be doubled or tripled.

Internet Coupons

- We gladly accept original paper internet manufacturer's coupons; however, no internet coupons involving any "free" products are accepted.
- With the purchase of three like manufacturer's products, we accept three Internet coupons, per store, per day.
- We do not accept internet coupons that do not appear to be originals or that will not scan.

Competitor's Coupons

- We gladly accept local competitors' paper manufacturer coupons for cents/money off of products. We also redeem circular, direct-mail, and register checkout coupons for money off of the total order. There is a limit of one per customer per day.
- If a coupon is marked as a Manufacturer's Coupon, we will accept it even if it comes from a Catalina coupon machine. Example: If the coupon is from Target, Food Lion etc. and has "Manufacturer's Coupon" printed on the coupon it is acceptable.
- We do not accept any internet coupons from other retailers.

•The Management Team in each store determines who their competitors are.

Rainchecks

•Rainchecks never expire and are accepted at any Harris Teeter store.
•We do not issue rainchecks for coupon items that may be out of stock or for "while supplies last" items.
•We reserve the right to limit raincheck quantities based on product availability and advertised limits.
•Rainchecks can be written for a limit of three or three "deals" unless otherwise stated in the ad.
•We do not reissue rainchecks for quantities not purchased at time of redemption.
•For deals where the pricing may vary, the customer must pay the highest of the amounts.

Scan Guarantee

•Our scan guarantees states "If an item scans higher than the shelf tag or sign, you will receive one like item free, excluding alcohol and tobacco."
•We will honor five "scan guarantees" per customer; all other pricing inadequacies will result in the difference between the shelf tag and the actual price of the item being refunded.

Harris Teeter reserves the right to limit quantities in coupon usage, as well as products and to amend our policies as we deem appropriate.

To better serve your shopping needs, please click here to view the Coupon Information Corporation's website for a listing of fraudulent coupons that will not be accepted at Harris Teeter. Join e-VIC and start saving!

Looking for more savings?

Join our e-VIC program to receive e-VIC Only electronic discounts, special rewards programs and a personalized weekly email notifying you when items you regularly buy are on sale! It's like having a personal shopper scan the weekly ad and identify your best deals. You can even build a shopping list to take with you to the store!

KROGER ~

NOTE: Coupons at Kroger (Coupons do not double here)

Unlike most grocery stores Kroger allows five coupons for the same item in one transaction. This is a plus for anyone who enjoys doing single transactions. Kroger is known for added sales directly to your card you must download them to your card to get the discounted item or sometimes a free item. Please visit Kroger.com weekly to receive your digital coupon. In order to receive sale prices, you must obtain Your Plus Card. If you do not have one, please go directly to customer service and they will give you one instantly. Kroger also known for having a great variety to offer their customers. They also have fresh sushi and an excellent salad bar.

Example:

Purchase 5 Showeet Toothpaste at $1.99

Use 5 manufacture coupons $1.00

Math

$1.99+5=$6.99

5x$1.00=$ 5.00

$6.99-$5.00 = $1.99 for 5 tubes of toothpaste

Store Coupon Policy
ON DIGITAL COUPONS www.kroger.com)

Customers who choose to participate in the digital coupon program are required to have a digital account with a valid, active Plus Card. Kroger Associates or partners are prohibited from setting up or otherwise maintaining a digital account not specifically linked to that Associate or the Associate's household. A valid Plus Card or an Alternate ID is required to access a digital account in order to use digital coupons at the time of purchase. Digital coupons and offers are deducted from a

Customer's total purchase prior to paper coupons or any other discounts, and cannot be added back or removed once the Card has been scanned.

•Limit 1 use per digital coupon, per transaction.
•Digital offers cannot be combined with paper manufacturer's coupons on the purchase of a single item.
•Digital offers do not double.
•A limit of 150 coupons can be loaded per household at any time.
•Digital reproductions of offers will not be accepted (such as using a mobile application to reproduce an image of an offer/coupon).
The store manager has the right to accept, decline or limit the use of ANY digital coupon or offer.

PUBLIX ~

NOTE: Coupons at Publix (some states double up to .50)

Publix is known for having "Stocking Spree's" which are sales that you must obtain from their store circular and/ or website. Please use your coupons to maximize your savings. They are also known for their Rewards this is an amazing program to pair with Stocking Spree Rewards you can earn a $10 Publix Gift Card for every $50 you spend on participating items just by submitting your Publix receipts on http://rewards.stockingspree.com Program Dates: 1/15/16-12/31/16. You must visit the website to see which participating items are on the list. Once you create your account, you'll be able to track your dollars spent and your rewards earned throughout the year. The more you buy, the more rewards you earn! Publix will allow you to stack their store coupon with a manufacture coupon. Which means you may use two coupons on one item. Use this to your advantage you should always try to match store coupons to manufacture coupons to maximize on your savings. You are allowed to use eight of the same coupons per day, per customer.

Example:

> Showeet Facial Scrub $2.68
>
> Buy (2) Showeet Scrubs
>
> Use 1 manufacture coupon save $3.00 when you buy 2
>
> Use 2 PQ Purple Flyer coupons that say save 1.00 dollar off of 1 (since you are purchasing 2 you may use 2 Publix coupons)
>
> Final Price $0 .36 for 2 Showet Facial Scrubs

Store Policy
Information located at www.publix.com

Publix is committed to helping you save money. We offer weekly specials, buy-one-get-one free promotions, and accept Publix, manufacturers', and competitor's coupons. When you add all these together, you can see why customers "Love to Save Here." So that all of our customers can benefit from these deals, we reserve the right to limit purchase quantities. The types of coupons we accept:

- Manufacturer's coupons, Publix coupons, Internet coupons, and coupons from nearby competitors (a list of which are posted at each Publix store).
- Coupons from competing pharmacies for prescriptions only.

Our acceptance guidelines:
- Acceptance is subject to any restrictions on the coupon.
- We only accept coupons for identical items we sell.
- We only accept a manufacturer's coupon and either a Publix or a competitor's coupon on the same item. Maximum of two coupons per item.
- Manufacturer's digital offers cannot be combined with manufacturer's paper coupons on the purchase of the same item.
- We do not accept percent-off-items or percent-off-total-order coupons.
- We do not accept coupons that Publix determines to be printed incorrectly. For example, a coupon missing a size requirement or other standard coupon details.
- We do not accept coupons presented via a mobile phone or device.
- We do not accept coupons that appear to be copied. All coupons must be originals.
- For a buy-one-get-one-free (BOGO) offer, each item is considered a separate purchase.
- We limit coupon redemption to eight of the same coupons per day, per household.
- Manager's approval is needed for individual coupons above $5.
- Dollars-off-total-order coupons will be limited to one Publix and one competitor's coupon per day, per household. The total order before coupons must be equal to or greater than the combined purchase requirements indicated on the coupon(s) presented. We consider competitor's coupons for dollars off groups of items to be a dollars-off-total-order coupon and will only allow one per day, per household.
- Money due back to the customer at the end of a transaction involving coupons will only be provided on a Publix gift card.

Our management teams will only issue rain checks for items which are advertised outside the store at a reduced retail. For example, on radio or TV, or in our weekly ad, co-op ad, mailer, or Internet site.
•We will only issue one rain check, per day, per household for an item.
•We will not issue rain checks for Publix, competitors, or manufacturer's coupons

BI-LO ~

NOTE: Coupons at BI-L0 (BI-LO will double coupons up to .60)

BI-LO is known for having affordable prices on select items they are convenient in most areas and they are a 24-hour grocery store. BI-LO is also known for fuel perks and gas savings. Take advantage of these gas savings and pair these items with manufacture coupons. In order to get the sales price, you will need to obtain a BI-LO BONUSCARD. Stop by the Customer Service desk at your local BI-LO store and fill out a registration form to get a BI-LO BONUSCARD instantly. It only takes a couple of minutes, and you can start using it to save on your purchases right away. You are allowed to stack Manufacture coupons at BI-LO with store coupons.

Example:

Showcet Pizza $2.99

Manufacture Coupon save $0.60 (remember coupons up to .60 double)

Store Coupon save $1.00

Math $0.60 x 2=$ 1.20

$1.20+$1.00= $2.20

$2.99-$2.20= $0.79

Store Coupon Policy
Coupon Policy located at bilo.com

General

•Store Management has the right to accept, decline, or limit the quantity of coupons and or items purchased in a single transaction or in a single day, by a single customer.

•BI-LO will accept manufacturer coupons (limit one per item), or BI-LO coupons (one per item), or valid internet coupons (one per item) or competitor coupons (one per item, with a limit of 10).

•Only original coupons will be accepted. Copies or coupons on mobile devices will not be accepted.

•To ensure product availability for all customers, BI-LO limits redemption to (5) five like coupons for the same item in the same day per customer. For example, if you have six of the same coupon and have purchased six items, we will only accept five of the coupons.

•A manufacturer coupon and a store coupon can be used on the same item in the same transaction.

•A manufacturer coupon cannot be used on the same item as an electronic coupon. An electronic coupon is linked to the Customer Reward Card and deducts automatically at the register when the required purchase is made.

•BI-LO does not accept any type of coupon for "Meal Deal or What a Deal" free items.

•The total coupon value cannot exceed the price of the item. No cash back will be given nor will cash back be applied to other purchases.

Competitor's Coupons

•BI-LO accepts competitor's BOGO coupons, one coupon per like item, per day, per customer.

•BI-LO accepts competitor's store brand coupons, one coupon per like item per day per customer.

•BI-LO will not match competitor advertised prices. The advertised offer must include the word "coupon" to be redeemed as competitor coupon.

•BI-LO will redeem competitor coupons for money off an entire transaction, one coupon per customer per day. BI-LO will not redeem competitor coupons for percentages off of order totals.

•Local competitors are defined as any grocery retailer in the local marketing area who sells like items. Coupons from club retailers such as SAM's, Costco, and BJ's will not be honored.

Doubling

•Only (5) five coupons on like items are eligible to double.

•Manufacturer coupons with a value of 60¢ or less will double, unless otherwise posted at store level.
•Double coupon redemption applies only to manufacturer coupons. BI-LO store coupons and competitor store coupons will not be doubled.
•Competitor coupons, coupons for free product, electronic coupons, coupons for alcohol/tobacco and coupons that state "do not double" will not be doubled.
See your local BI-LO store for more details. • Effective September 28, 2014

FOODLION~

NOTE: Coupons at Food lion (Coupons do not double)

Make sure to sign up for the Food Lion MVP Card to get the sale prices and download e Coupons that come off at checkout. Some locations allow stacking store coupons with manufacturer coupons Foodlion is known for have great sales on their frozen foods and well as their beauty products. Feel free to visit their website at www.foodliion.com to load coupons directly onto your MVP card or print them from home. Foodlion will accept up to ten like coupons per transaction.

Example:

Showeet Frozen Vegetable on sale $2.00

Use ten $1.50 manufacture coupons

Math

$2.00 x 10= $20.00

$1.50x10=$15.00

$20.00-$15.00= $5.00

Coupon Policy located at www.foodlion.com

Food Lion accepts manufacturer and store coupons that can be obtained from newspapers, flyers, the internet, our MVP Savings Center, foodlion.com, or our Catalina coupon machines at each register.

*Certain exclusions and exceptions apply. See below for details.

Coupons must meet the following requirements:

• We will accept paper coupons or coupons loaded directly to your personal MVP card
• Coupons must be in date
• The purchase requirements of each coupon must be met
• Coupons with specified limits must be followed
• The coupon value will be deducted from the final retail (regular or MVP) and cannot exceed the final sale price of the product
• Only one coupon is allowed per item
• A maximum of ten (10) of the same coupon can be used when ten (10) of the specified items are purchased. Any coupons downloaded on your personal MVP card counts towards the maximum of 10
• We will accept paper or internet coupons that appear to be the original, with the exception of "FREE "internet coupons
• We will accept "FREE "coupons when they are not printed from the internet

EXCLUDED COUPONS

Food Lion will not accept the following coupons:

• "FREE" coupons printed from the internet
• Coupons that appear to be altered in any way
• Competitor Coupons
• Food Lion does not double or triple coupons
• Coupons that are displayed on a phone or tablet

SHOPPERS FOOD ~

NOTE: Coupons at Shoppers (coupons double up to .99)

Shoppers is known for having affordable prices as well as having great sales on seafood items. While Shoppers doesn't have a savings card they do have an app you can download directly from the play store onto your smart phone. Once you select the digital coupon you would like to use give your cell phone to the cashier so they can scan your digital coupon. Shopper is also known for mailing $ 10.00 off $50.00 coupons directly to your home, please check your weekly mail. Shopper will only allow 4 like coupons per transaction. Each store reserves the right to only allow four like coupons per day it's strictly up to management. If you have more than four coupons and they allow you to use four more of the same coupon you will have to do it in a separate transaction. Remember slow and steady sometimes wins the race.

Example:

Purchase 4 Showeet Cakes for $1.99

Use 4 Manufacture Coupons for $0.95

$1.99 x4= $7.96

$0.95x4= $3.80 x2 = $7.60

Total Cost for 4 Showeet Cakes $0.36

Store Coupon Policy
Information located at www.shoppers.com
· SHOPPERS will double the value of valid manufacturers' coupons with a face-value of up to 99¢ (example: 25¢ = 50¢, 50¢ = $1.00, 75¢ = $1.50.)
· Valid manufacturers' coupons with a face-value of $1.00 or greater will be redeemed at face-value only (example: $1.00 = $1.00, $1.50 = $1.50, $2.00 = $2.00.)

· The value of the "doubled" manufacturer's coupon may not exceed the retail price of the item. If the price of the item is less than the "doubled" value of the manufacturer's coupon, the item will be free.

· Buy One, Get One Free coupons will NOT be doubled.

· Manufacturers' coupons may be obtained from the newspaper, mailers or Internet.

· Coupons must contain valid redemption information and a valid bar code (UPC) to be honored.

· SHOPPERS reserve the right to limit manufacturers' coupons eligible for "doubling" purposes to four (4) identical coupons.

· Manufacturers' coupons that state "Do Not Double" or "Not subject to Doubling" will be redeemed at face value only.

· Photocopies of coupons are not acceptable.

· SHOPPERS reserves the right to refuse any coupon deemed to be fraudulent and the right to change or terminate this policy at any time.

MY PRACTICES ON CERTAIN COUPONS ~

- Buy two save $1.00 or buy 2 save $2.00 or by 3 save $3.00 coupons. I wait to use these type of coupons when stores have a sale like "buy one get one free" or "buy one get one half off."
- Buy one get one free coupon. I find sales at stores that say, "buy one get one free." Purchase two and both items will be free.
- $1.00 -$2.00 Coupons use during any super double event.
- $ .75 coupons, wait until the product is on sale for $2.00 or less. I will use this coupon at a store that doubles making the coupon worth $1.50.
- Pay attention to store sales that say buy three save $3.00 or purchase five save $5.00 these are good indicators that coupons may exist on these sale items.

Additional

- Don't forget to price match at stores like Family Dollar, Walmart, and Target. You can also use coupons and store coupons on top of price matching.
- Don't forget the point system at Rite Aid and Walgreens. They are not same but points = money you can use on future purchases.
- Store coupons that say save $10.00 when you spend any amount. May be used at other stores like Harris Teeter and Giant check with your local store.
- Gas points come in handy. Purchase multiple items that have gas points to lower you bill at the pump.
- Federal Holiday means no coupons that week, use this time to straighten your stockpile and prepare for the weeks ahead.

> Internet coupons can only be printed two per device.

MISCELLANEOUS TIPS FOR THE NEW COUPONER ~

Rebates after you in store purchase from Catalina's, Ibotta, Saving Star and More

What is a Catalina? ▯

A Catalina is a coupon that is printed at the register at participating stores when you purchase select participating items. The Catalina coupon prints out from the Catalina machine at the register at the end of checkout. Always make sure the Catalina machine is on (look for a green light). Before you start your transaction you can always ask the cashier to verify that the machine is indeed on. The best way to find out about Catalina promotions is through the website at▯Catalina.com. Often times they are advertisements for upcoming promotions.▯

If your Catalina didn't print, you can head to their website here to fill out the form http://support.catalinamarketing.com▯and they will mail you the Catalina right away. The process is easy.

Ibotta (information taken directly from Ibotta.com)

Ibotta is a fun and easy way to earn real money just for buying your favorite products. You can earn $20 or more each time you use the app. It's easy. Learn about products by taking polls, reading facts or watching short videos - you choose how much or how little. It works in 50 plus national grocery chain restaurants, with new stores being added all the time. It's fast.

Get your money within hours of taking a photo of your receipt. Download the app and earn extra savings

Savings Star (information copied from savingstar.com)

Save money on your groceries with exclusive freebies, healthy offers & BIG savings on your favorite brands. Earn cash back on your online shopping too! Go to savingstar.com and scroll through this app before your shopping trip to select products for extra saving.

RAIN CHECK/RC ~

This is what you get from customer service when an item is out of stock for you to be able to get the deal at a later time. Some rain checks do expire so make sure you look at the expiration date on your rain check. You can use coupons when you redeem a rain check. Customer Service will write a limit on the rain check. They will ask you how many items you want. Always tell them the maximum allowed. If you want more than what they have allotted for that day go back tomorrow and ask for another. Repeat the process until they have them in stock or you are satisfied by the amount you received. Make sure to redeem that rain check before your coupons and rain check expire. (Not sure if your store allows rain checks?) Ask they will let you know.

COUPONS OFFERED VIA TEXT ~

American Eagle Outfitters Text the word JOIN to 32453 and you'll receive coupons via text message.

Arby's Text the word ARBYS to 27297.

Auntie Anne's Pretzels Text PERKS678 to 21333

Babies R Us Text BABIES 9 to 30364

Bath & Body Works Text the word BBW to 588229

Bed Bath & Beyond Text OFFER to 239663

Domino's Pizza Text the word DOMINOS to 366466

Dunkin' Donuts Text the word PERKS to 386546

Famous Footwear Text the word PROMO to 326687

Fashion Bug Text the word BUGBYTE to 50799

IKEA Text the word JOIN to 62345

JC Penney Text the word JOIN to 527365

Kmart Text the word KMART to 414141

Kohl's Text the word SAVE02 to 56457 to join the text club.

Lord & Taylor Text the word SALE to 95555

Macy's Text the word CPN to 62297

Old Navy Text the word ALERTS to 653689

Payless Shoes Text the word SHOES to 747474

Qdoba Text the letter Q to 50500

Redbox Text the word SIGNUP to 727272

Sears Text the word SEARS1 to 595959

Subway Text the word SUB to 782929

Target Text the word COUPONS to 827438

Toys R Us Text the word DEALS to 78697

COMPANIES TO REQUEST COUPONS TO BE SENT TO YOUR HOME

VOILA ALFREDO CHICKEN 1 800 563 1786

VIENNA SAUAGE 1 800 528 0849

GERBER JUICE 1 800 511 6862

NESTLE WATER 1 866 599 8980

WELCH'S JUICE 1 800 340 6870

SUNNY DELIGHT 1 800 395 5849

FRUITY PEBBLES 1 800 431 7678

COFFEE MATE 1 800 637 8534

DUNCAN HANES 1 800 362 9834

BREAKFAST MILK 1 800 289 7313

LEAN CUISINE 1 800 993 8625

SMARTONES 1 800 762 0228

STOUFFERS 1 800 225 1180

TGIF CHICKEN 1 800 457 9810

V8 FUSION JUICE 1 800 871 0988

CAMPBELL'S SOUP 1 800 257 8443

WISHBONE DRESSING 1 800 343 9024

KEN'S RANCH DRESSING 1 800 545 5707

KRAFT DRESSING 1 800 847 1997

SMACKERS JELLY 1 888 550 9555

SAMPLE LETTER TO MANUFACTURES REQUESTING COUPONS

Dear (enter companies name)

Hello my family and I really enjoy (enter product here) (tell them what you like about the product) due to some recent changes in our finances we must stick within our food budget. I know coupons would help us achieve our goals and I am writing this letter to see if you would please mail any coupons or samples to my home? I would also like to be placed on your mailing list for any upcoming coupons. I thank you in advance for your time.

Sincerely,
(Enter your name)
(Enter your address and email address)

WHERE TO MAIL EXPIRED COUPONS
Let's help our military families

Support Our TROOPs®⃝
P.O. Box 70
Daytona Beach, FL 32115-0070
Coupons must be divided into perishable/ nonperishable before mailed.

NUMBERS TO CORPORATE OFFICES

BI-LO: 1-800-768-4438

CVS:⬚1-888-607-428

Dollar Tree: 1 877-530-8733

Family Dollar1866-377-6420

Food Lion:⬚1-800-210-9569

Giant: 1-717-249-4000

Harris Teeter:⬚ 1-800-432-6111⬚

KROGER: 1-866-221-4141

Meijer's: 1 877-363-4537

PUBLIX: 1-800-242-1227

Rite Aid:⬚1-800-748-3243⬚

Safeway: 1-800-723-3929

SHOPPERS: 1-855-SHOPPERS

Shoprite: 1-800-746-7748

Target:⬚1-800-440-0680⬚

Walgreens:⬚1-877-250-5823⬚

Wal-Mart:⬚1-800-925-6278⬚

Weis: 1-866-999-9347

GLOSSARY

MQ/Manufacturer Coupon: ⬚Coupons issued by manufacturers

OOP/ Out of Pocket: Your actual cost, what you spent in dollars

IP/Internet Printable:⬚Coupons found on various internet sites

NLA/No Longer Available:⬚This means a coupon or deal is not available any more

SS/Smart Source:⬚One of the coupon inserts typically found in the Sunday paper (Comes out 3 or 4 times a month)

RP/Red Plum: One of the coupon inserts typically found in the Sunday paper (Comes out o3 or 4 times a month)

PG/ Proctor & Gamble: One of the coupon inserts typically found in the Sunday paper (Comes out monthly)

YMMV/ Your Mileage May Vary: ⍰You may have to travel to another store to score the deal ⍰

QUICK RECAP ~

Ok now you have enough to information to start couponing. I suggest getting comfortable with one store at a time and it would be wise to learn the store policies. I would also suggest starting out small – do one deal at a time and four coupons at a time.

As you gain confidence in your couponing abilities it will be easier to broaden your knowledge at your next grocery store. Don't forget to plan out your shopping trips. If you can go to three stores within a five mile or so radius while you're already out, you should attempt to coupon while you're already out. Don't waste gas going back and forth between stores and home. Use your gas wisely; remember, your whole goal is to save in every area possible. Don't forget to price match at participating stores. Only use your coupons on sale items, do your homework and find the best sale available.

DONATIONS

If you live in the Metropolitan area and you would like to donate. Please consider Dee's House of Hope
http://deeshouseofhope.org/

✟ THE ULTIMATE SAVING ✟

Now I want to ask you one last question? You've sat and read this entire book, you've allowed me to save you and your family money on your grocery bill. I want to also introduced you to JESUS let him save you from an eternity without HIM.

Repeat this prayer out loud:

GOD I accept your son JESUS as my personal LORD and SAVIOR I believe in my heart and I confess with my mouth that JESUS is LORD. I believe HE died on the cross and you raised HIM from the dead. Thank you for cleaning me, I repent of my sins. Thank you for accepting me into your Kingdom.

If you read that prayer aloud congratulations heaven is rejoicing over, you. I am so happy you made the decision to accept CHRIST as your personal LORD and SAVIOR. I prayed the same prayer myself fourteen years ago. Now find a local church and grow in the kingdom of GOD. If you live in the Maryland, DC, Virginia Area I invite you to my church Spirit of Faith Christian Center one church many locations please visit www.spiritoffaith.org to find the nearest location.

Made in the USA
Columbia, SC
12 February 2018